Conducting a Contact Center Assessment

Published by Online Customer Care
P.O Box 122
Glen Gardner, NJ 08826

ISBN-13: 978-1481865272
ISBN-10: 1481865277

First Edition: January 2013
Printed in the United States of America

Table of Contents

List of Tables 9

List of Figures 11

Introduction 13

    Why conduct an assessment? 13

    Structuring a contact center assessment 14

    What elements should an assessment contain? 16

    How long should an assessment take? 17

    Strategic Alignment 17

    How can the assessment be customized? 20

Discovery 25

    Areas of Focus 25

    Functions 26

    Classifications 27

Efficiency 29

    Operations 31

    Considerations 31

    Visualizing Disparities in Performance between Groups 34

    Analysis of Variance (ANOVA) 36

    Additional Benchmarks 38

Workforce Management 41

    Considerations 41

    Relevant Questions 48

Table of Contents

Process Management 51

    Considerations 51

    Relevant Questions 54

    Process Management – Data 55

    Examples of relevant processes 59

Effectiveness 61

    Customer Relationship Management 63

    Considerations 63

    Relevant Questions 66

    Knowledge Management 69

    Considerations 69

    Relevant Questions 75

    Quality Assurance 77

    Considerations 77

    Relevant Questions 79

Capability 83

    Human Resources 85

    Considerations 85

    Contact Center Agents – A Composite View 97

    Relevant Questions 98

    Information Technology 101

    Considerations 101

    Relevant Questions 103

    IVR 105

    CRM System 106

    Knowledge Management System 108

    Business Intelligence 111

Differentiation 116

Table of Contents

Relevant Questions 118

Simple Benchmarking 118

Value Perspective 119

Comparative Performance 121

Assessment Outputs 124

Considerations 126

Output Example 131

ROI Analysis - Example 136

Comparative Analysis 139

Customer Satisfaction Survey 143

Employee Satisfaction Survey - Example 147

Unusual Outputs 150

Contact Center Design Guidelines 151

Ergonomic Design Considerations 154

Conclusion 158

Glossary 160

Index 166

List of Tables

Table 1 - Assessment Drivers, Goals and Requirements 20

Table 2 - Potential QA Tasks... 79

Table 3 - Contact Center Supervisors – A Composite View.................. 95

Table 4 - Contact Center Agents – A Composite View 98

Table 5 - Example of an IT Evaluation of CRM System 107

Table 6 - Contact Center Competitive Differentiation........................... 118

Table 7 - Contact Center Value Perspective 119

Table 8 - Comparative Matrix Example - Best Practice........................ 123

List of Figures

Figure 1 - Assessment Discovery and Opportunity 28

Figure 2 - Boxplot Examples 35

Figure 3 - Example of ANOVA Output.. 36

Figure 4 - Benchmark Cost by Contact Center Type 39

Figure 5 - Mapping Customer Relationship Management – Example.... 68

Introduction

This book is intended for managers and analysts who want to assess a contact center's operations and identify opportunities for improvement. As such, much of its focus is on the people, process and technology that are used to operate the center.

It would be unrealistic to proclaim that any guide dealing with contact center assessments can cover every scenario or emulate the many outstanding publications on individual aspects of customer service support, such as workforce management, customer relationship management, quality assurance, and so on. As such, the goal of this book is to provide a framework for an end-to-end assessment of the contact center, to include guidelines for gathering key information and presenting findings.
.

There is enormous variation in every contact center environment and this, coupled with the plethora of reasons that motivate the perceived need for an 'assessment', means that it is virtually impossible to create a standardized template for conducting such an assignment. However, regardless of the specific intent, there are certain questions that must be answered, certain information that must be analyzed, and certain observations that must be made in order to baseline findings and recommendations for each function within the contact center.

Why conduct an assessment?

There are several reasons why a company may wish to conduct a contact center assessment. Most are intended to articulate ways to cut costs while improving, or at least maintaining, customer satisfaction. Some are motivated by dysfunctional mergers or problems with the operation of geographically distributed centers. Many involve start-up companies who are struggling to define 'world class' customer service. Some assessments focus on specific functional areas, such as workforce management, while others are intended to pave the way for the implementation of new technologies.

Managers usually have specific reasons for wanting a contact center assessment, including:

- How to decrease the number of abandoned calls
- How to provide a framework for employee skill and training feedback
- How to manage cost per contact for maximum efficiency
- How to improve customer satisfaction through contact quality
- How to incentivize and retain agents
- How to improve average speed of answer
- How to balance agents with busy hour volumes
- How to meet the management demand for cross-selling
- How to recover from service disruptions.

Whatever the reason, the boundaries of the assessment need to be clearly defined and agreed upon by all concerned. Too many assessment findings end up being 'swept under the carpet' or ignored due to a nebulous statement of work or lack of senior management involvement. Conducting an assessment without these up front insights is dangerous, because it leads to unrealistic recommendations.

The biggest challenge in conducting a contact center assessment is not the collection of data, but in establishing logical connections that generate meaningful insights. It's not difficult to generate reams of data and findings, especially from a contact center, but without a mutually agreed upon business goal, this will offer very little in terms of pragmatic application.

Structuring a contact center assessment

Contact centers today often represent the pulse of the business, handling orders as well as customer service issues. As such, the contact center culture, policies and procedures, operating environment, and future vision must be aligned with the company's overall business strategy. At its most basic level, a contact center assessment should identify any opportunities for improvement in this regard.

Sometimes, a contact center assessment involves building a business case for the implementation of a new technology which promises to reduce contact time while providing sophisticated customer relationship management tools. However, even a limited contact center assessment will usually identify several other avenues for improvement in the areas of efficiency, effectiveness and capability.

Most contact center managers today are faced with having to do more with less, and an assessment can help to pinpoint how this can be achieved. By examining workforce scheduling, human resource management and training practices, knowledge management and end-to-end processes, adjustments may be identified that do not require significant capital investment. This is the often the 'low hanging fruit' that can be implemented in a matter of days rather than months or years.

The ultimate goal of any contact center assessment should be to review the 'as is' state of the business, operations and technology environment, and to create a roadmap which enables management to assess the feasibility of attaining the 'should be' ideal based on an understanding of best practices and clearly defined opportunities for improvement.

In order to conduct an assessment that realizes a logical roadmap for improvement, it is crucial to first identify broad areas of focus, and then identify the functions and classifications which relate directly to those focal points. By taking this approach, the assessment will reveal significant opportunities for improvement that may cut across several 'siloed' functions and classifications, rather than producing disparate recommendations that fail to 'connect the dots'.

The ultimate output of any assessment should clearly reveal the contact center's ongoing commitment to customer service excellence and contribution to the achievement of 'best-in-class' business practices.

What elements should an assessment contain?

Method	Impact	Cost	Value
Interviews	Highest	Highest	Highest
Focus Groups	High	Medium	Medium
Observations	Low	Low	High
Surveys	Low	Medium	Medium
Documentation	Low	Low	High
Data	Lowest	Lowest	High

Interviews are typically a primary source of strategic and tactical information gathering during an assessment. These should be focused on all levels of management, not just within the contact center, but also with the executives responsible for the day-to-day running of the business. Questions in these interviews should be geared towards gaining an understanding of the perceived strategic and tactical role of the contact center, potential opportunities for improvement and future vision.

Focus Group sessions may be conducted separately with both experienced and novice front line CSRs, as well as supervisors and specialist groups. The goal of these sessions should be to ascertain the 'pulse' of the contact center and identify ways in which customer and employee satisfaction may be improved.

Observations are an unobtrusive way of gathering procedural and qualitative information on customer interactions and day-to-day work tasks at the contact center. This should ideally include side-by-side contact and work monitoring that involves both human and systematic actions.

Surveys may be used to gather both customer and employee feedback as part of the assessment. The goal of such surveys should be to identify 'big ticket items' that may be affecting the strategic and tactical goals of the contact center.

Documentation examined as part of the contact center assessment should include processes, policies and procedures, and reference and user guides.

Data is available in abundance at most contact centers and can be utilized to pinpoint opportunities for improvement in key areas such as workforce management and cost per call.

How long should an assessment take?

Depending upon the scope of the project and, to a lesser extent, the size of the contact center, a partial assessment may be conducted in one business day or a full-scale effort may take a matter of months. In general, the discovery phase should take no longer than five to ten business days on site. However, assessment outputs as a result of discovery will take three to five times due to the volume of data and other information that needs to be assessed prior to formalizing opportunities for improvement and business recommendations.

Strategic Alignment

An overarching consideration of any assessment is how leadership and management strategies are reflected by contact center operations and how these may be better aligned. Understanding how business strategy currently impacts contact center operations and how it may affect the implementation of any opportunities for improvement is ultimately critical to the perceived value of the assessment.

As such a logical first step in any full-scale assessment is to baseline the company's business strategy as this pertains to the contact center and to identify any perceived opportunities for improvement in this regard based on interviews with senior management. For example, is the contact expected to provide insights that help the business achieve competitive advantage? Where does the contact center fit in to the company's value chain? Does management believe that the center can be further optimized? Does the center adequately coordinate with the rest of the business to provide seamless customer service? Is the center doing a good job of conveying strategy to the front lines? Does strategy permeate every aspect of contact center operations?

Strategic insights must influence the entire assessment, both in terms of discovery and recommendations. By showing the link between the purpose of work and the strategy for achieving business goals, the assessment will realize its maximum potential.

Regardless of the scope of the assessment, it's important to start by getting some answers regarding the perceived role of the center pertaining to business strategy.

The following are examples of 'kickoff' questions which could be directed towards senior management:

- What is the company's mission and vision and how do these affect the contact center?

- How does the company's overall approach to business impact contact center operations?

- How is the return on investment (ROI) of any functional, procedural or media changes that impact the contact center environment measured?

- How does the Information Technology strategy impact the achievement of best-in-class contact center operations in the following areas?

    - enterprise architecture planning and implementation
    - application procurement and integration
    - unified communications and reporting
    - customer relationship management
    - single-source knowledge base development and maintenance
    - technical support and change management
    - disaster recovery

Introduction

- How does the company's business approach affect the following:

  - The <u>functions</u> that the contact center supports (e.g., sales, marketing, billing, collections, etc.)
  - The <u>processes</u> that the contact center supports (e.g., escalation paths, trouble ticket resolution, knowledge management, etc.)?
  - The <u>media</u> that the contact center supports (e.g., calls only, social media, web forums, etc.).

- What <u>metrics</u> are considered by management to be the most important in the day-to-day operation of the contact center?

- Are current management reports sufficiently integrated to enable meaningful business intelligence to be gleaned and disseminated?

- What constraints, if any, does budget allocation currently place on contact center operations?

- In terms of strategic importance, how do you perceive the Contact Center's role vs. the rest of the organization?

- Corporate Plans for the contact centers (consolidate/eliminate/decentralize)?

- What business goals does it support (revenue, retention, satisfaction, decreased dependence on outside vendors)?

The answers to these questions will provide the basis for a more informed contact center assessment.

How can the assessment be customized?

Business Drivers	Goals	Requirements
Customer Satisfaction	Resolving on First Contact	Empower agents Improve Training
	Maximizing access	Provide multi-channel access Improve scheduling Increase staffing Reduce contact time
Cost Reduction	Minimizing contact time	Provide rapid system response Provide intuitive system design Provide outstanding content Facilitate data gathering
	Minimizing turnover	Improve screening Provide incentives
Market Intelligence	Gathering customer data	Conduct customer surveys Provide contact tracking
	Conducting root cause analysis	Provide analysis tools

Table 1 - Assessment Drivers, Goals and Requirements

The question is which of the requirements listed in the preceding table are relevant to this particular contact center assessment? What does the assessment sponsor really want to get out of this initiative? While it appears obvious, failure to recognize the underlying intent of the assessment from the outset can result in a significant waste of time and money.

The following considers several potential recommendations that may result from an assessment, each of which is considered in more detail within this publication.

Improving Customer Satisfaction and Reducing Cost

Empowering Agents

Many contact centers rely on an initial period of classroom training to provide agents with the in-depth knowledge required to resolve a customer problem on the first point of contact. In technical environments, or those which handle a wide spectrum of customer interests, this has resulted in a segmented work force and, arguably, an increase in the number of escalated contacts due to misdirects (e.g., the customer selected the wrong prompt and was routed to an agent who was not empowered to resolve their inquiry). This approach also encourages inconsistency as agents interpret training recollections into a customer response. Despite the proliferation of written reference materials around the agent's desktop, many find it virtually impossible to find the right information at the right time. Apart from random monitoring, the absence of systematic information sharing can mean that busy agents have little or no way of assessing whether or not they are giving the customer the optimal response. Such a goal can be most consistently and cost effectively achieved by providing a constantly updated and easily accessed online information retrieval system which provides not only answers to technical problems and billing/general inquiries, but also management approved guidance on issues such as product returns and complaints.

Minimizing Contact Time

It seems reasonable to assume that customer access to a contact center can be maximized by reducing the amount of time each agent takes to resolve a particular customer problem or inquiry. Reducing contact time is not only a potential customer satisfier, therefore, but can also contribute directly to cost reduction by enabling agents to become more productive in terms of the number of customer contacts handled. Of course, a great deal depends upon the approach to minimizing contact time. Abruptly escalating calls after five minutes talk time or terminating conversations after giving customers incomplete answers may indeed contribute to a decline in contact time, but will also result in a far higher number of callbacks (and a subsequent decline in customer satisfaction). The ideal situation, therefore, is to not only reduce contact time, but also to ensure that the customer is satisfied with the response.

Providing Rapid System Response

The provisioning of rapid system response is a critical technical issue which can "make or break" an online customer service system. Several seconds delay is far more than a minor irritation to an agent who is attempting to placate an impatient customer. The simple fact is that unless the system responds to an agent command within what is considered a *reasonable* period of time, the system will be regarded as more of a hindrance than a help and the agent will devise personal workarounds which may or may not be optimal. Even if system content is outstanding, poor response time will render it useless to time-pressured employees. Interestingly, a time lapse is probably more acceptable to the customer who is interacting with a Web site or Interactive Voice Response unit, than with another human being. Customers clearly expect immediate and articulate advice from agents - not an uneasy silence.

Providing Intuitive System Design

Rapid system response must of course be accompanied by an intuitive system design. Users should be able to quickly navigate through an *integrated* customer service system which provides all of the functions required to answer routine problems and inquiries, in addition to gathering data relevant to the customer contact. Process improvement, workflow or task analysis, rapid prototyping and usability testing are all critical elements of good system design, yet these are often neglected by those development groups whose only goal is to produce a system which more or less meets high-level business requirements within the constraints of time and budget. In such cases the absence of strong cooperation between management, users and system development results in a functional system which does little to improve agent productivity and can even diminish customer satisfaction.

Providing Outstanding Content

Content maintenance is the bane of many customer service environments. No matter how fast and how intuitive the system may be, the absence of accurate, relevant and complete content information will ensure its downfall. Troubleshooting systems which cover only a small percentage of known customer problems, user instructions which are poorly written and presented, scripts and online help applications which serve only to confuse the user, and policies which no longer reflect management initiatives, are all indicative of a system which was deployed under the misguided assumption that technology alone would provide some sort of "magic bullet", rather than to interactively assist users by adhering to continuous improvement processes. Reducing cost and increasing customer satisfaction means that a user can immediately retrieve the information they need in a way that makes sense to them. If the information isn't available, then a management-driven quality improvement process will ensure that it is there in the future.

Facilitating Data Gathering

There are two reasons to collect data on customer contacts. The first is to keep an historic record of the transaction so that it may be recalled should the customer be engaged in future contacts with the company. The second is to gather market intelligence which may be used to identify opportunities for improvement with regard to the company's product or service. Properly documented customer inquiries, problems, complaints and suggestions can clearly help marketing and product management teams understand ways in which they can gain new customers while retaining the existing base. More often than not, however, customer comments are obscured by inconsistent and unclear data gathering techniques, and further impeded by systems which fail to facilitate analysis of that data, leading to an obscure mass of information which does little more than fill storage facilities. Unstructured manual note-taking by agents, for example, is often a counter-productive exercise which contributes to significant after call work and has a detrimental effect on customer access. A customer service system must facilitate automated and interpretable data gathering wherever possible.

Ultimately, the assessment must be geared towards the needs of the business and contact center environment, as well as strategic goals. Obviously, every center more or less varies in terms of industry, business function, size, customer type, budget, resources, and level of management support. As such, any assessment must consider the practices that most influence a particular contact center's day-to-day operational environment.

Discovery

Once the scope of the assessment has been defined, the first step is always the process of discovery, whereby 'tools' such as interviews, focus groups, data collection, observation and surveys are used to gather the baseline information which will ultimately become the assessment output. It is also important to remember that an assessment is a situational analysis, and is not intended to be a vindication of a pre-ordained course of action, such as the deployment of a new CRM system. Strategically, a full scale assessment should ultimately reveal the value of the contact center (cost/benefit), the purpose of the center (mission, vision), and also consider the return on investment (ROI) the center realizes for the business.

Areas of Focus

There are four areas of focus that represent the highest level of assessment output at a functional level:

Focus	Definition
Efficiency	Providing service at optimal or close-to-optimal productivity and costs.
Effectiveness	Providing a level of service consistent with the customers' and business expectations.
Capability	Structural, organizational or operational factors that influence the current and future effectiveness and efficiency of the center.
Differentiation	Identifying opportunities for improvement via understanding of competitive practices.

A major 3/

Functions

At the functional level, the contact center can be broadly categorized into customer-facing, support, and analytics. Customer-facing functions include anything to do with customer contact routing and handling. Support functions include systems, management, forecasting, scheduling, training, etc. – in other words, any aspect of contact center operations that provides support to those who deal directly with the customer. The third function is analytics – the metrics and reports that are used to reveal business intelligence and operational efficiency outputs that can help to control costs and retain customers. Other elements that impact the contact center, such as facilities, may also be considered, depending on the scope of the assessment.

Function	Definition
Customer-facing	End-to-end customer interaction with the contact center, including the routing and handling of contacts from any medium.
Support	Process management, policies and procedures, workforce scheduling, knowledge management, information technology and human resource management
Analytics	Analytics should include consideration of operational metrics, return on investment, business and competitive intelligence.

Classifications

The most granular level of an assessment dissects contact center functions into their related classifications.

Classification	Definition
HR	Human Resource management, including hiring, promotions, training, supervision, and empowerment.
WFM	Workforce Management, including forecasting, scheduling and real time control of center efficiency.
CRM	Customer Relationship Management, including segmentation, satisfaction and retention.
KM	Knowledge Management, including creation and maintenance of all internal/external information sources.
PM	Process Management, including definition, measurement, analysis, improvement and control.
QA	Quality Assurance, including all monitoring, feedback and quality improvement initiatives
IT	Information Technology, including assessing the contact center's ability to provide fully integrated multi-channel and customer-centric service and business intelligence.
OPS	Operations - day-to-day management of the contact center.

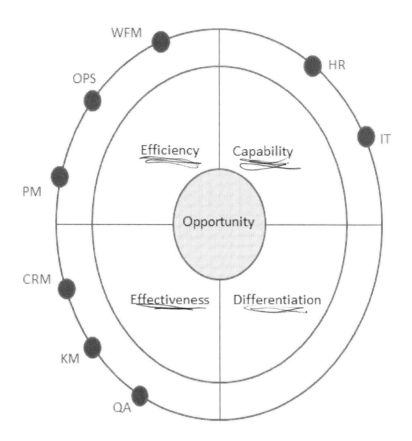

Figure 1 - Assessment Discovery and Opportunity

Classifications belong primarily in the areas of efficiency (i.e., workforce management, operations, and project management), effectiveness (i.e., customer relationship management, knowledge management, and quality assurance), and capability (i.e., human resources and information technology). Differentiation is subjective and can involve any or all of these classifications.

The next section explores the elements discovery and analysis in each area of focus and associated classifications.

Efficiency

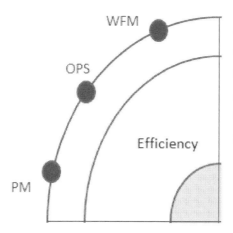

Efficiency in the context of a contact center assessment is defined as providing service at optimal or close-to-optimal productivity and costs.

There are three particular classifications that impact contact center efficiency. These are workforce management, operations and process management.

Evaluating efficiency typically involves analyzing significant amounts of data generated from contact center ACDs and comparing the results to industry benchmarks and/or contact center best practices. Depending on the size of the center, this type of analysis may involve a breakdown of aggregated data to the individual or group level. Observation leading to in-depth task analysis can also help to identify day-to-day operational inefficiencies. Understanding how supervisors and agents perform their respective jobs on a given day may provide clues as to which policies and procedures, as well as overall managerial expectations, make sense from both a cost and customer perspective.

This section also contains several key indicators of critical contact center metrics, as well as typical benchmarks pertaining to operations and costs.

OPS

Operations

Considerations

By definition, Operations are a support function mainly focused on the efficient day-to-day running of the contact center. The goal of this section is to baseline the operating environment and understand disparities in performance through high-level data analysis.

There is usually no shortage of operational data available at the contact center. Typical focal points for managers are average speed of answer, abandonment rates and contact times. Complex measures such as resolution on first contact, occupancy and cost per call should also be focal points.

Other methods of gathering assessment information include management interviews and observation sessions. Key operational questions are listed below.

Relevant Questions

Question
Total Number of Contact Center FTE's (% Full Time / % Part Time)
Supervisor to Agent Ratio
% Of Time Spent on the Phone (and direct after call follow-up)
% of Time Spent in Meetings and Training
% of Time doing Research, Paperwork (Not including call wrap-up), and special projects

Efficiency

Question
% of Time Available
% Agent allocation (Service Calls, Inbound Sales, Outbound Sales, Order Fulfillment, Other)
What are your metrics for responding to social media-generated issues?
Total compensation (Agents / Supervisors)
Costs associated with the support and maintenance of contact center applications.
Total Telecommunications Costs
Training Costs
Other costs directly attributed to contact center operations (furniture, leasing, utilities, etc.)
Total *accounts* served?
Total *households/institutions* served?
Total *active accounts* (those having one or more transactions per year) served?
Total number of incoming service & sales contacts (IVR & Agents) *offered*?
Total number of incoming service & sales contacts (IVR & Agents) *handled* (used in cost per contact calculations)?
Total number of outbound sales contacts handled?
% Contacts handled by IVR alone?
% Contacts handled by an Agent?
% Contacts handled by an Agent following IVR access?
% of agents taking Inbound contacts only
% of agents taking Outbound contacts only
Average times per inbound/outbound contacts
Contact breakdown by type and by medium
Average service level for inbound calls
Different target service levels for different customers?
Goal: Percent answered in seconds
Actual: Percent answered in seconds
Different target sales service levels for different customers?
% inquiries answered on the first call, regardless of whether the customer is transferred or is placed on hold (ROFC)?
% total offered calls are dropped from the queue (abandoned calls or abandonment rate)?
% Abandon rate?
% customer calls blocked?
Queue time (in seconds)
Average number of years of education past high school for agents?

Operations

Question
Agent turnover rate?
What is the average tenure of agents?
After how many months is an agent considered at the peak of their skill level?

Detailed Questions

Question
What are the top issues faced in managing this Contact Center (consolidation, service, satisfaction, compensation, motivation, morale, vendor support, complaints, staffing)?
Who is responsible for your social media strategy?
What kind of revenues, if any, is the contact center generating and how are these measured (e.g., revenue per call vs. cost per call)?
How is the contact center budget structured (% for resources v. Information Technology v. facilities)?
How do you determine cost per call?
How does the contact center compare to the competition or benchmarks in terms of cost per call?
Do you listen to customer feedback via social channels?
Have you determined particular skills agents need to deal with social media? If so, what are these?
Do you have a social media standard operating procedure? Where does this reside?
What service level agreements, if any, exist between the Contact Center and other organizations? What is the impact of not meeting these agreements (decrease in customer satisfaction, lost revenues, etc.)?
How do you coordinate multi-channel customer contacts (chat, email, calls, web forums, twitter, fax, mail, etc.)?
Do the existing contact center disaster recovery processes satisfy you? Why?
Are you aware of any plans to expand the scope of Contact Center functions? What are the ramifications of this?
What do you feel are the advantages of union vs. non-union CSC environments (if relevant)?
Are there costs in your budget that you feel should be allocated/shared elsewhere (e.g., Information Technology)?
Where are the biggest bottlenecks that can impact the perceived service level at the contact center (e.g., escalations, field issues, technology, etc.)?

Question
Do you measure Resolution on First Contact? If so, how do you define this metric (e.g., no transfers, one transfer, one callback)?
How useful are the management reports you receive? How could these be improved?
What are the things you enjoy most about working at the center (e.g., co-workers, customer contact, challenge, empowerment, problem-solving, etc.)?
What are the strengths of the center (e.g., teamwork, dedication, customer orientation, technology, knowledge, centralization, etc.)?
What are the weaknesses of the center?
Do you think that centralization is a good idea?
Opportunities for telecommuting?
Primary drivers behind centralization (growth, restructure, complaints, suggestions)?
Opportunities for outsourcing?
What is the manager to agent ratio?
Annual center budget - likelihood of increase/decrease?
Projections for growth (contact volume, agents, facilities, revenue via center)?
Current best practice perceptions and why?
Are there plans to expand the scope of center functions?

Operations - Data

Visualizing Disparities in Performance between Groups

One useful exercise in any contact center assessment is to visualize disparities in performance between like groups or individuals in order to identify opportunities for improvement. An intuitive tool for accomplishing this is the boxplot.

Operations

A boxplot is defined as a data display that organizes data values into four parts using the lower extreme, lower quartile, median, upper quartile, and upper extreme measures of performance:

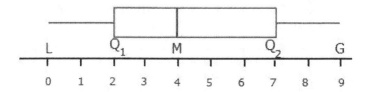

Here is an example of using the boxplot to depict average talk time by group:

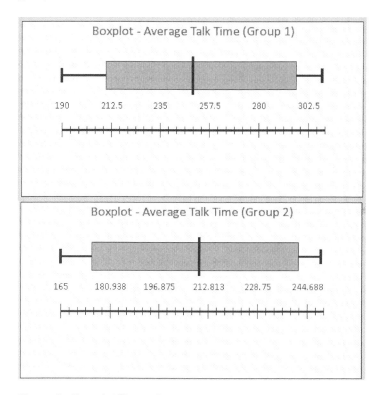

Figure 2 - Boxplot Examples

Efficiency

In this example, the boundaries of each box represent the 25th and 75th percentile scores for each team. The tips of the whiskers represent the maximum and minimum values. The line within the main box represents the median value. For a given team or individual, therefore, the extremities indicate the maximum and minimum talk time values for that person or the members of that group. The wider the gap between the whiskers, the greater the variability and potential loss of efficiency within the group.

Analysis of Variance (ANOVA)

In large contact centers, a more formal statistical analysis procedure is the Analysis of Variance (ANOVA), which is used to determine whether the difference in performance between teams is statistically significant.

Team	1	2	3	4	5	6
1		x	x	x	x	x
2	x			x	x	
3	x					x
4	x	x				x
5	x	x				x
6	x		x	x	x	

Figure 3 - Example of ANOVA Output

This example demonstrates a statistically significant difference in performance for a particular measure between Groups 1 and 6 and most of the other groups at the center. Teams that are significantly different from a large number of teams need to be investigated in more detail (the ANOVA output could be construed as positive or negative in terms of performance – the table simply indicates a significant difference). In other words, less variability between teams (i.e., blank cells) indicates greater conformity to a norm.

A focal point of most contact center assessments is the analysis of performance measures. With reams of data being automatically collected every day by ACDs, it isn't unusual for system-generated reports on simple metrics such as abandonment rate, average speed of answer and average talk time to become the focal point of the entire contact center operation. Compound metrics, such as average handling time, cost per call, and especially service level give more insight into how well the center is run, while measures such as resolution on first contact (ROFC) are at least as important, but more difficult to ascertain.

Example – Typical operational 'rules' for a contact center:

- ACW = < 30 seconds
- ASA = 20 seconds Abandonment > 10 seconds = <2%
- Agents Total Talk Time (ACD) Average = 5.25 hours per day (65% of paid time). AUX = Group Meetings, Training & Development, and Project Management Time
- Average Handling Time per call < 180 seconds
- Average Service Level = 85% (i.e., percentage of calls answered in 20 seconds or less)
- Service Level must stay above 75% (including calls placed on hold), else overflow to designated staff.

Measures typically used to evaluate contact center costs

- Cost/call
- Cost/representative
- Cost/sale
- Comparison to expense plan
- Cost of acquisition
- Cost/customer
- Cost/revenue unit

Measures most often used to gauge center access

- % Calls abandoned
- % Calls answered in "x" seconds
- Average Speed of Answer
- % time busy.

Additional Benchmarks

Category	Low	Mean	High
Annual Budget			
% Costs for HR			
% Costs for Telecommunications			
% Costs for Hardware/Software			
Weekday hours of Operations			
Weekend hours of Operations			
Agent available time			
% contacts handled by IVR			
% contacts handled by agents			
% contacts handled by internet/e-mail			
% contacts handled by inbound Fax's			
Cost/call			
Cost per minute			
# inbound calls per year			
# outbound calls per year			
Annual inbound minutes			
Annual outbound minutes			
# Agent seats			
# FTE Agents			
Turnover rate			
% outsourced calls			
% perfect customer satisfaction score			

Operations

Another approach to measuring contact center efficiency is by
benchmarking specific areas of focus, as follows:

Focus	Cost/call	Cost/ minute	Cost/ Agent	% perfect score
Orders				
Call Routing				
Pre-Sales				
OB Telemarketing				
Market Research				
Customer Satisfaction Surveys				
Technical Support				
Complaint Resolution				
Dispatch				
Customer Service				

Figure 4 - Benchmark Cost by Contact Center Type

WFM

Workforce Management

Considerations

Workforce management is a key classification within the realm of contact center efficiency. The goal here is not to conduct an exhaustive analysis of all historical data using sophisticated software, but rather to understand the challenges facing workforce management analysts (if this position exists) at the contact center in terms of forecasting contacts and scheduling agents to meet service level requirements.

While the Internet has changed the dynamic of customer interaction significantly, the telephone still remains the primary medium for customer communication with most contact centers today. Of course, there are now service levels for social media, email and chat, but the big hitter when it comes to workforce management at the majority of contact centers is the number of calls answered in x seconds.

How Workforce Management Issues typically affect service levels

- Service level issues are typically caused by one or more of the following factors:

    - Inaccurate forecasts
    - Ineffective queuing of calls
    - Insufficient staff employed to answer calls

- Scheduling issues
- Inefficient skills-based routing of calls
- Inadequate call handling times.

Any complexity in the day-to-day operating environment amplifies all of these issues. Particularly when it comes to insufficient staff employed to answer calls, some simple math at the onset of the assessment can help to demonstrate typical workforce management issues (in this case specific to inbound calls), as follows:

- Average Talk Time: x seconds
- Average After Call Work: y seconds
- Average calls offered per day (z)
- Total call handling time: x*y*z
- Total agents (a)
- Average agent occupancy time per day time (b)
- (x*y*z) / (a*b) = Total time each agent is needed to handle all calls offered each day

For the busiest contact centers, the number of minutes required to handle calls offered is often much higher than the number of minutes that the agents are occupied.

For the purposes of assessment, if time permits it is useful to consider conducting a 'date in time' study that examines exactly what happened from a workforce management perspective on a specific day at the contact center when service plummeted to unacceptable levels in terms of average speed of answer and abandonment rate. Such a study will potentially provide key information as to accepted WFM and staffing practices that are detrimental to the efficient running of the center – practices that may not be evident on a "normal" day, but which can have a detrimental effect on customer satisfaction and even retention in the long run.

'Date in Time' Studies

The correct scheduling of staff is a science that could provoke endless hours of mathematical debate. Contact centers that are large enough to use workforce management software to forecast and schedule staff rely largely on sophisticated algorithms that work with historical data in order to correctly staff the center to optimal levels at all times.

During the busiest hour on the busiest day of the week, unless the center has unlimited resources, service levels are bound to drop. In many tightly staffed centers, service levels don't just drop during this time - they often *plummet*. Savvy workforce managers who have to report on service levels by the day realize that much of this drop can be salvaged by hitting 100% service levels through overstaffing earlier or later in the day. Whether acknowledged or not, this is standard practice at many centers, especially those that employ fulltime staff.

Of course, it is never that straightforward either, unless the center employs a 'universal rep' concept, whereby any agent can answer any contact. Most high volume centers use skills-based routing, whereby agents can be members of several groups based on their training and considered level of competence. So five skill codes means five service levels that can be rolled up into one overarching statement of fact (e.g., "80% of the telephone contacts were answered within 20 seconds on this date in time").

The following slides depict an example of a simple – with apologies to the purists - 'date in time' assessment when service levels dropped below 10% for a prolonged period, causing over 400 calls to be abandoned in one hour alone. However, it should be noted that the <u>overall service level for the day exceeded target and the call forecast for the day was 97% accurate</u>.

**Key Question #1 –
Was the Call Forecast Accurate?**

- Comparing historical data to the call forecast

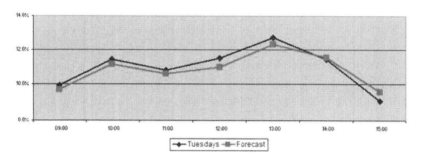

This chart indicates that the combined call forecast for this particular date in time
was somewhat lower than historical data for preceding Tuesdays.

The call forecast as shown above looks slightly low, based on previous
day-of-the-week historical data, but perhaps not enough to trigger any real
concern.

Were Hourly Call Forecasts Accurate?

- The hourly forecast follows the historic trend
  - Exceptions are the unusual absence of a significant
    mid-morning spike and an extreme spike after midday.

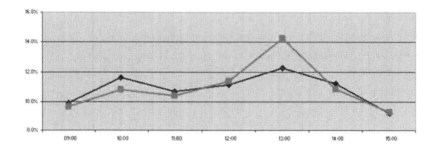

The hourly call forecast also followed historical trends, but as depicted by the lines above, had no obvious precedent for the spike that occurred around 1:00 p.m.

Next, take a look at the skills-based routing configuration:

Forecast Accuracy by Skill

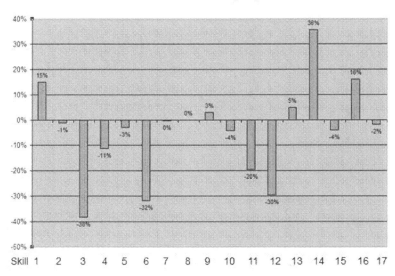

The fact that <u>no less than 17 skill groups existed</u> for a center that offered basic services is cause for alarm regardless of forecast accuracy. However, the center could still have handled the unusual spike were it not for the extraordinary inaccuracy of the forecast when it came to those skill types. Several skills were off by over 30%, as shown in the previous slide. In effect, based on skill code designations, certain agents were actually idle when service levels plunged to 10%.

Another factor that contributed to the disastrous meltdown at 1:00 p.m. was the fact that the majority of agents were scheduled for lunch breaks at or around that time:

Key Question #2
Were sufficient agents staffed to answer forecasted calls in a timely manner?

- Could changing break schedules have helped?

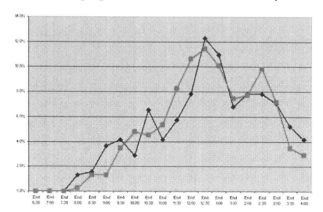

Further investigation of individual agent performance within skill groups also showed that those agents designed to codes that rarely received calls, but which handled complex cases, had huge variations in talk time and after call work time.

Key Measures

While many metrics are used in day-to-day contact center operations, few are more important than **occupancy**. This can be defined as the percentage of time an agent is working on customer contact related activities, whether directly with a customer or in an after call work state. A textbook definition of this metric in a thirty minute period is Call Volume * Average Handle Time / Number of Agents * 1800.

In contact centers with high call volumes, it is not unusual for agents who are being held to very high occupancy levels to seek ways in which to alleviate the pressure of constant customer calls by using different call states and other tactics in order to gain a 'breather'. There are several ways of achieving this without drawing overt supervisory attention, including:

- Staying on the line (in ACD mode) after transferring a caller to another party
- Picking up a call from the queue and then dropping it immediately
- Going into ACW mode for 15-30 seconds after every call, regardless of whether there is a need to do so
- Switching from AUX to ACW to AUX to ensure that the agent's name does not rise to the top of the queue
- Staying in ACW immediately before a scheduled break.

In order to alleviate this behavior, some contact center managers assign specific periods of 'closed key' time for agents to catch up with outstanding tasks throughout the course of the day. The key questions in making the decision whether or not to implement closed key time in a contact center are (a) how are customers affected by batch processing of work? And (b) does the batching of ACW time offer more control than letting agents use the after call work state as appropriate after each call?

If closed key time does not exist at the contact center being assessed, then depending on the transactions being conducted by the company, the following possibilities could be considered:

- New customer set-up
- Prospective customer quotes
- Billing adjustments
- Invoice copies
- Product tracing
- Filing
- Customer satisfaction surveys
- Outbound sales calls
- Social Media and Email responses

Workforce management studies have demonstrated that in centers where some contact types require 5-10 times the normal handling time, service levels are very sensitive to the contact mix during peak hours. For example, depending on the size of the contact center, taking one agent out of the available state for thirty minutes can cause a ripple effect across the entire center by adversely impacting the average speed of answer and consequently the overall service level.

Relevant Questions

Question
What are your key metric targets (service level goals, occupancy, abandonment, ASA, talk time, ACW)? How do you ensure these targets are reached?
Does your workforce management forecasting and scheduling include considerations of social media coverage? If so, what are these?
What are your off-peak vs. busy hour statistics (e.g., Queue Times, Blocked Calls, ASA, Transfers, Escalations, Abandonment)?
Is a "blended" call configuration used (e.g., reps in outbound mode switch to inbound based on calls in queue)? What are the business rules around this?
What is the most selected function in the IVR? What frequency do other selections report?
% of Escalations
% of calls handled by IVR
Blocked calls
Scheduling for multi-channel customer contacts?
Percentage of multi-lingual calls? Which languages?
What is the incidence of holds during calls? Why do you think this occurs?
Are you aware of any user tasks that could impact the workforce model?
How do you staff for specialist groups? How many of these calls are routed automatically? Via a separate 800 number (DNIS)? Via a front line rep?
How many transactions (multiple tasks) occur per call, to the best of your knowledge?
Do you measure conformance / adherence? Why or why not?
How can the contact center consistently meet service goals?
How can customer transactions be streamlined?
How can contacts be routed most effectively without manual intervention?
How can forecasting and scheduling be optimized to avoid contact delays?
How can front line groups be better aligned to handle contacts?
Was the overall contact forecast accurate? If so, were expected service levels maintained?

Question
What was the overall variation in service levels by interval (30-minutes, one-hour, etc.)?
What was the overall variation in service levels by skill type (common contacts/lower talk time, etc.)?
Were sufficient agents staffed to answer forecasted calls in a timely manner?
Were calls allocated correctly?
Are your contacts routed to skill groups based on specific customer needs (e.g., billing, orders, technical support, etc.)? Why?
How much consideration has been given to allocating agent 'closed key' time to conduct follow-up work? Why?
How does the contact center differentiate each contact for routing, handling and reporting purposes (i.e., by product or service, customer segment, agent skill, menu selection, etc.)
What media types does the contact center handle (i.e., phone, email, chat, forums, twitter, web)?

PM ●

Process Management

Considerations

Process Management is another area that can significantly impact contact center efficiency. In the course of an assessment, it is not unusual to find reams of detailed flowcharts in obscure locations, such as storerooms or beneath empty desks. These documents probably represent the efforts of a small group of individuals whose task long ago was to brainstorm how to handle various types of customer contact. Depending upon the mix of people and time constraints, this may have resulted in detailed descriptions of internal technical support and billing inquiry processes, a relative absence of cross-organizational processes, and a cursory mention of content and knowledge maintenance processes.

In large organizations, which may have several contact centers fulfilling various purposes, the employment of a different process modeling methodology and content classification for each one is common, depending upon the original motivation of the design team. The sentiment expressed by the project manager might be that "it doesn't matter what anyone has done before, we're going to do it the 'proper' way and it's up to them if they want to rework their process flows and bring everything into line". In other words, unless the assessment reveals a company-wide imposed standard, cross-organizational process development and maintenance can resemble a contemporary "Tower of Babel".

Normally, process owners are assigned to significant areas of concern, such as billing inquiry, credit and collections, troubleshooting, reservations, etc. While the most elaborate processes may be designed for these areas, it is not unusual for key customer service operations processes to be overlooked until such incidents arise. Take, for example, the customer who insists on calling the call center back before the deadline for their commitment is scheduled to be met. In the ideal world, of course, this should never happen, and it may well be that the customer contact process owner may have only created a process which visits this contingency at a very high level. Failure to fully describe the repeat customer callback process, however, can create a debilitating situation in which agents may take several courses of action, such as erroneously calling a supervisor, creating a secondary commitment, or warm transferring the call to the originating agent. This is just one example of several processes which are more difficult to define after operations have commenced, if only because the original process owners have been deployed elsewhere and no one else has the time to fully investigate the situation.

Here are some of the other processes which are often overlooked in the foundation of a new contact center environment:

- Service Realization
- Online Content Updates and Maintenance
- Knowledge Acquisition and Engineering
- Interactive Voice Response Scripting and Functional Support
- Online and Offline Escalations
- Change Management
- Root Cause Analysis of Inbound Contacts
- E-mail and Social Media Support
- Online Help Maintenance
- Online Scripting
- Mail Logging and Routing.

Several of these processes require far more than nebulous agreements. Service Realization, for example, often means that the marketing and sales groups have some way of notifying customer service of any new activities which might impact customer contact volumes and inquiries. Yet it is not unusual for this process to be compromised by tenuous links between marketing and customer service.

Also worthy of particular consideration is the fact that it is not always apparent from disparate process maps exactly what the scope of potential contact transfers, escalations, commitments and after call work (including manual workarounds such as remote faxing, etc.) really involves. By eliciting information on those contacts which are not likely to be resolved at the first point of agent contact, the contact center manager can evolve a "real world" picture of those contingencies which are likely to adversely impact service levels. For example, if detailed investigation of the troubleshooting process reveals that of the fifty problem types defined, twenty two are likely to result in callback commitments, the center must construct the workforce model to reflect this contingency. At the same time, the assessment could examine each potential callback type and determine whether or not the agent's inability to resolve a particular contact immediately will be due to empowerment constraints, training shortfalls, or technological inadequacies.

By conducting this type of root cause analysis, management can then take whatever steps are necessary to avert repeat customer calls and outbound callback commitments. If it is determined that certain contacts are being escalated because their content is so cryptic that the agent was never trained in that area, then it is contingent upon management to ensure that the online knowledge base contains this information in a format that is easily followed. If other contacts are being escalated because these involve some degree of decision-making ability, then management need to conduct a cost/benefit analysis to ensure that the inability of a front line agent to credit a few extra dollars to a customer's account is not seriously affecting service levels. Clearly defined processes will also allow customer service management to determine exactly how long each transaction should take, thereby performing a "sanity check" on the workforce management model.

Here is a framework* that could be used by a contact center in order to set up a process management team:

- Step 1 - Form Process Management Team
- Step 2- Implement VOC/Customer Satisfaction Survey
- Step 3 - Identify the service elements most critical to customers
- Step 4 - Set satisfaction targets and performance levels for the key critical elements
- Step 5 - Perform analysis to measure baseline performance
- Step 6 - Report current performance using balanced scorecard
- Step 7 - Select improvement initiatives that addresses the most critical service elements
- Step 8 - Set performance improvement targets for the current cycle
- Step 9 - Perform improvements
- Step 10 - Bring improved process under control
- Step 11 -Verify that improvement goals have been achieved
- Step 12 - Repeat steps 5 through 11 for the next improvement cycle

*with thanks to my colleague Rohit Ramaswamy, PhD, author of 'The Design and Management of Service Processes' for his input.

Relevant Questions

Question
Does the contact center use documented processes? Where are these located?
What kind of process metrics are in place to support the contact center? Is a data collection plan in place to support these metrics?
Are policies and procedures applied at the contact center? If so, who is responsible for maintaining these?
Are agents expected to adhere to specific processes when handling contacts? If so, how are these conveyed (e.g., training, online workflows, documentation)?
Do any process improvement teams exist at the contact center? If so, how do these teams convey and Implement their findings?
How are processes prioritized for improvement (e.g., customer impact, budgetary limits, performance status, business impact, etc.)?
Does the contact center use a process improvement framework to support the implementation of improvements?
Has the center conducted a voice of the customer survey to

Question
determine perceived process shortfalls? If so, how does customer feedback impact process management?
Has the center performed any previous analysis to measure baseline process performance?
Does the center use any type of a balanced scorecard approach?

Process Management – Data

The assessment should include a review of existing contact center processes and a clear understanding of the methodology used. For example:

- Describe the process
- Determine the process boundaries
- Flowchart the process
- Document technical, procedural, and organizational issues
- Document interfaces and feedback loops
- Relate customer expectations to the process
- Establish in-process metrics
- Establish direct measures of quality
- Gather process cost information
- Report efficiency, effectiveness and change status.

Here are the types of tools that could be used in an assessment of process management and their purpose:

- Histograms - to study the spread of key process variables, such as AHT
- Pareto Charts - to identify the "critical few" causes of a problem (such as high ACW times)
- Scatter Plots - to determine relationships between key variables (customer satisfaction and service levels)
- Trend charts - to evaluate trends over time
- Cause and effect (fishbone) diagrams - to identify
- Control charts - to determine whether process performance is under control.

Efficiency

Control charts compare the performance of continuous or discrete variables against statistically computed "control limits". The idea of control limits is that the performance of any process is inherently variable. There are some sources of variability that occur due to *identifiable* causes - for example, the variability in AHT might come due to incorrect ACW practices on the part of some agents - other sources are just random, for example due to unpredictable variations in call mix. The trick to managing a process is to understand when variability occurs due to random causes and when it occurs due to identifiable causes, so that energy is not spent in investigating every little deviation from the average or target value. The control chart allows this to occur. The control limits on a control chart, calculated form historical data, represent the range of normal random variation. Points outside these limits are described as "out-of-control" and need to be examined in greater detail, because the likelihood of these points varying to this extent just due to random causes is extremely small.

Consider the control chart for ACW on the next page. The two lines at 9 and 11 represent the control limits. The chart shows that the pick-up ACW time varies from week to week, sometimes going up and sometimes down. For most weeks, this is due to normal causes of variation and stays within the control limits - however, on week 5 the ACW time exceeds the control limits and should be examined in greater detail.

Process Management Charts

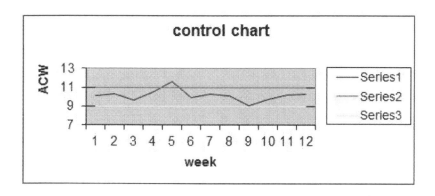

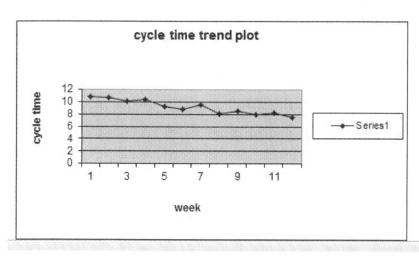

Process Management Charts (continued)

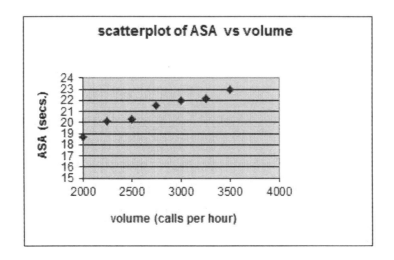

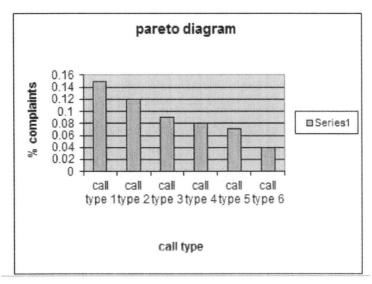

Examples of relevant processes

Operations

- New Product/Service Support/Marketing Activity Notification
- Disaster Recovery (Loss of Telephone or Computer Network)
- Customer Contact Root Cause Data Gathering & Analysis
- Customer Satisfaction Data Gathering & Analysis
- Facilities Management
- Screening and Hiring
- Partnership and Service Agreements
- Customer Service Quality Analysis & Improvement
- Agent Appeals
- Agent Rewards and Recognition.

Information Support

- Interactive Voice Response (IVR) Customer Script Maintenance
- Initial and Continuation Training
- Methods & Procedures Information for Customer Contact Handling
- Agent Help System Support (For Customer service Systems)
- Agent Script Development and Maintenance
- Content Development for New Product/Service ("How To")
- Content Maintenance for Existing Product/Service ("How To")
- Problem-solving Support for New and Existing Product/Service (Knowledge Acquisition/Engineering).

Systems Development & Maintenance

- Interactive Voice Response (IVR) Functional Improvements
- Systems Change Request – Prioritization and Implementation
- New Systems Definition, Prioritization and Implementation
- Database Administration
- Systems Administration.

Customer-Facing

- Routing Inbound Customer Calls to Appropriate agents
- Classifying, Routing and Responding to:

  - ➢ E-mail Messages
  - ➢ Chat Requests
  - ➢ Fax Messages
  - ➢ Voice Mail Requests
  - ➢ Web Communications
  - ➢ Social Media

- Handling Customer Account Maintenance, such as:

  - ➢ Change customer address
  - ➢ Change pricing plan
  - ➢ Renew or cancel contracts
  - ➢ Modify credit limit
  - ➢ Change billing responsibility
  - ➢ Record customer comments

- Handling Customer Orders and Reservations, such as:

  - ➢ Inventory location
  - ➢ Credit approval
  - ➢ Price negotiation

- Resolving Billing Inquiries, including:

  - ➢ Pricing Inquiries (customer)
  - ➢ Request for Invoice Copy
  - ➢ Change Billing Cycles
  - ➢ Explain feature charges
  - ➢ Create revised or on demand bill
  - ➢ Explain taxes

- Handling Customer Complaints
- Handling Misdirected Calls
- Online Escalation of Customer Calls
- Handling Customer Initiated Callbacks.

Effectiveness

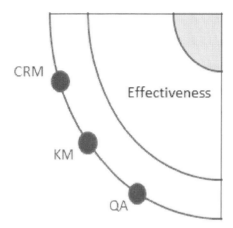

Effectiveness in the context of a contact center assessment is defined as providing a level of service consistent with the customers' and business expectations.

There are three particular areas of focus when it comes to contact center effectiveness. These are customer relationship management (CRM), knowledge management (KM) and quality assurance (QA). This section explores each of these assessment focal points in detail.

CRM

Customer Relationship Management

Considerations

NOTE – Systematic considerations for Customer Relationship Management are covered in the Capability – Information Technology section.

Contact center assessments that focus on customer relationship management sometimes result in the following findings:

- Supporting systems that are so poorly designed, integrated and maintained that agents use them only because they are compelled to do so
- Supporting materials so cryptic, irrelevant or outdated that that they prevent agents from giving correct, timely answers
- Augmentative technologies, such as Interactive Voice Response, implemented in a way more detrimental than helpful to customers
- Web-based service perceived by customers as unnecessarily intrusive and time-consuming
- E-mails remaining unopened as dual-tasking agents are reassigned to handle massive inbound call queues
- Customer care environments unable to gather, analyze, respond and react to useful business intelligence data.

So what would the optimal CRM assessment finding look like? Perhaps something like this:

- Multichannel access -- e-mail, web chat, web callback, voice-over net, voice-over IP, social media monitoring, web collaboration, etc.
- Integrated knowledge management and contact management tools
- Personalization of every customer interaction
- Unified off-the-shelf computer-telephony integration
- Legitimate customer knowledge through superior business analytics and market intelligence.

Of course, most contact centers fall somewhere in between the sublime and the ridiculous. In order to assess where a particular center stands in terms of CRM, there are certain questions that need to be answered from the outset.

- *Does the customer relationship management system facilitate interaction with the customer?*

  Perhaps the most complex challenge facing online customer service today is deploying or maintaining systems which facilitate frontline agent interaction in stressful circumstances. For the contact center agent, perhaps that means a utilizing an off-the-shelf CRM application that integrates the contact tracking system with the online documentation, trouble ticketing, billing, customer callback, and troubleshooting applications.

  Anyone who has observed contact center agents using homegrown systems has probably witnessed the scrolling of interminable lists while deciphering to which category a particular customer contact belongs, or seen agents spending several minutes of after call time writing voluminous notes (which most often are used only for contact history purposes, rather than as a viable source of business intelligence), or retyping the same information several times because the application is poorly designed. Certainly, the agents can learn how to work with the system, but how much time is being wasted on unnecessary tasks, and what effect is that having on customer satisfaction?

- *Is it easy to find the right information?*

Even superbly designed customer relationship management systems often do nothing more than create elaborate placeholders for content. If the user cannot find the information that they are looking for quickly, then they may dismiss even the most sophisticated systems as useless. It is pointless implementing integrated systems if users have to perform unnecessary or cryptic tasks in order to resolve the customer's needs.

Those responsible for acquiring information, composing it, and ultimately presenting it online should always position themselves as close to the user as possible. Just as a system designer is responsible for ensuring that the system is easy to use, the knowledge engineer is responsible for ensuring that information is easy to find. Contact center agents may tend by nature to be more tolerant than customers in general.

- *Is the information understandable?*

Perhaps a company boasts about its carefully designed CRM or knowledge management system. Perhaps it is remarkably easy to find the right information. Perhaps the only question that remains for the contact center agent is "Can you comprehend the information as it is presented?" This contingency highlights the critical content issues of style, vocabulary, legibility, presentation, and interpretation. For the agent who is "dual processing" (i.e., listening to the customer while trying to understand the information on the screen), this task is key to increasing productivity. The faster the agent can assimilate and even convey the information as presented, the sooner the call will end.

- *Is the information accurate?*

This question illustrates not only the necessity for continual feedback loops within an organization, but it also highlights the importance of rapid content maintenance. Just as the contact center agent does not want to retrieve obsolete price plans, the customer does not want access a company web site to read about a promotion which ended yesterday. The processes for gathering information (a.k.a. knowledge acquisition) and developing robust and timely information update channels across an organization are key factors in the successful implementation of online customer service

Relevant Questions

Question
How do you feel that the company can improve its customer relationships?
How important is the sales function in the Contact Center? If relevant, how do you support this?
How supportive are field personnel of the contact center structure? What can management do to optimize this relationship?
What is your complaint handling process? How do you believe you can reduce the volume of complaints?
How can the company do a better job of managing customer expectations?
How effective is your complaint handling process? Do you conduct root cause analysis?
How do you feel about the balance between formality (metrics-driven) vs. customer satisfaction-driven management practices at the contact center? How can this be improved, if at all?
What channels do you provide for gathering customer satisfaction data (e.g., random calling, mystery callers, informal polling during call, IVR, e-mail, postal, fax, telephone surveys, focus groups)?
Do you practice customer profiling based on inputs from the fields and/or CSRs? Why or why not?
What do you think of current customer segmentation practices, if any?
How satisfied do you feel that customers are with your ability to answer their questions?
How satisfied do you feel that customers are with the IVR, web, queue times, EDI, fax, postal and e-mail support?
Opportunities for segmentation?
Has the concept of the "customer" and the relative impact of its component parts been fully understood and accepted from the business perspective?

Question
Are the business processes that facilitate the meaningful dissemination and analysis of client information in support of strategic goals clearly defined?
Is there strategic buy-in to the notion of sharing cross-organizational information in order to nurture long-term client relationships?
Do all customer-facing groups (including sales and marketing) understand the relative value of universal customer recognition?
Is the current and forecast volume of customer transactions and consequent administrative support functions supported by the CRM solution?

Effectiveness

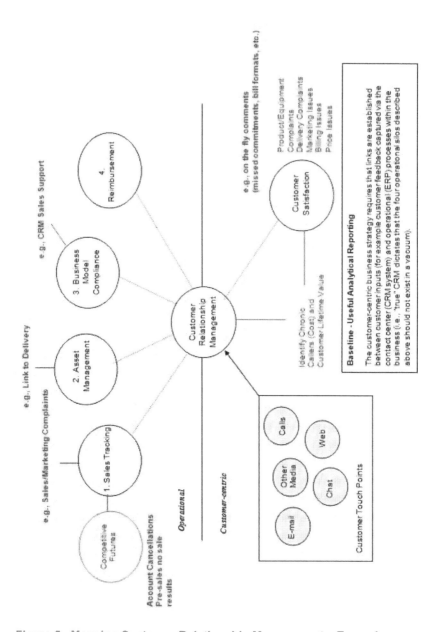

Figure 5 - Mapping Customer Relationship Management – Example

KM

Knowledge Management

Considerations

For assessment purposes, it is important to consider that a knowledge management system in the context of a contact center – whether comprised of straightforward html scripts on the web or a sophisticated off-the-shelf application – is usually designed to augment and sometimes replace more traditional forms of information sharing, such as classroom training and offline resources. The question to be answered is just how effective this approach is in terms of both center operations and customer satisfaction.

Most trainers don't have the luxury of keeping new agents in the classroom for what might be considered an adequate period of time. Instead, they have to contend with diminishing budgets, increasing competitiveness and more demanding customers. Hard-pressed contact center managers are usually judged more on accessibility metrics than the often intangible benefits of allowing agents to attend training on the latest product upgrade or service enhancement.

Typically, contact centers provide a certain amount of "on-the-job" training for new agents. This normally involves working alongside an experienced agent or subject matter expert who is capable of coaching the new agent as they handle customer contacts. This practice is useful in helping to reinforce any classroom training the new agent might have received, in addition to familiarizing the agent with what are considered the standard practices of the contact center. During this period, the new agent is given strong indicators as to how the best performers handle customer inquiries and complaints. In customer service environments that do not require the agent to ensure consistency and accuracy of content information by first validating their response through reference materials, the experienced agents may rely solely on their own knowledge and respond to the customer accordingly. Even in centers where management do request that agents validate their responses, reference materials (whether on paper or online), are often so poorly maintained that even if the agent does find a reference, it may be completely outdated, cryptic or incomplete.

Subjectivity of response becomes most evident in troubleshooting scenarios, where experienced agents may be able to pinpoint a problem within seconds, while newer agents struggle with their outdated and poorly designed materials, or sift anxiously through the "cheat sheets" they or their peers composed during on-the-job training. If the option is available to them, new agents in this predicament will put the customer on hold and attempt to retrieve the answer by asking any available peer. As a last, but not uncommon resort, the agent will advise the customer that their problem needs to be handled by a specialist or technician. At this point, the agent will attempt to escalate the call. If no "internal help desk" agents are available, a callback time frame is arranged with the customer. In the meantime, several minutes have elapsed, leaving only a dissatisfied customer, a perplexed or embarrassed agent, potentially several more minutes of after call work (scheduling the follow-up, creating a trouble ticket, and composing a note about the customer's problem), more work for an already overburdened internal help desk group, and a drop in the contact center's service level.

Some contact centers encourage agents to listen to internal help desk agents resolving customer problems, particularly in the case of online transfers. While this practice appears to make sense, it is a reactive process which clearly does not involve information sharing across the agent population. In other words, the only one to really benefit is the agent who happened to receive the call that resulted in the contact escalation. This sort of selective information sharing is endemic in customer service environments who have failed to make knowledge management a priority.

The task of ensuring that reference materials are updated and distributed in a timely manner is both daunting and time-consuming, especially in large or distributed customer service environments. Even in organizations which have employed a team of technical writers to ensure that paper documentation is kept up to date, a secondary problem emerges - the documentation is so abundant that finding the right information at the right time is highly improbable.

In summary, implementing and maintaining a knowledge base often requires not only a significant amount of analysis and design, but depends upon substantial management commitment in order to succeed. Too many knowledge management systems become the brunt of users' criticism as a result of poorly planned implementation and virtually non-existent maintenance practices. The success of any knowledge management system is contingent on meeting business requirements, some of which may have been derived from the overall goals of the customer service environment. For example, a contact center manager with the goal of increasing calls *resolved on first contact* from 78% to 90%, while *reducing average handling times* by 40% may use a combination of these metrics in addition to savings on materials and reductions in training costs to determine the return on investment from a knowledge management system. The original business requirements might have included the following:

The knowledge management system will:

- Present a structure and interface which is intuitive to any user
- Automatically capture specific user interactions for root cause analysis purposes
- Automatically capture data for contact tracking purposes
- Retrieve information that is relevant to the customer inquiry or problem
- Respond to user search requests within x seconds
- Retrieve information that is easily understood
- Retrieve information that is complete
- Retrieve information that is accurate.

For many customer service environments, the decision to implement a knowledge management system represents a paradigm shift from the days in which a clerical worker would drop a few sheets of company policy directives on the desk of each agent, or a technical writer would spend six months preparing or updating a user manual. Yet in an age of commodities and demanding customers, few can afford to be complacent. Rapid, satisfactory answers to customers inquiries and complaints can not only improve customer service operations, but can also encourage customer loyalty even while gathering market intelligence and establishing intra-organizational feedback channels.

The following contact center knowledge management components could be used as a baseline for the assessment:

- Standard Operating Procedures
- User instructions
- Online help
- Correspondence templates
- Scripts
- Knowledge Bases
- Error messages
- Training guides
- Reference documents
- IVR scripts.

Ideally, a knowledge management system will encompass the following essential properties:

- *Accessibility*

  Accessibility is a measure of the *speed of response* and *ease of use* of the knowledge management system. Speed of response may include the time taken to initiate the system and the time taken to respond to user input, such as a database search. If either of these mechanisms are unreasonably slow, leading to user frustration or stress, the system is likely to be rejected as unusable. Contact center management must ensure that in-process metrics driven by best in class scenarios constitute the minimal acceptance criteria for speed of response.

Ease of use is a term usually applied to the human factors issue of making system usage intuitive to a user. For the purposes of a knowledge management system, this would involve elements such as searching, information structure and presentation, and automatic data capture. A cumbersome user interface can cost precious seconds at the agent level, and is especially detrimental at the direct customer interaction level (e.g., the Internet), where it can result in calls to customer service which should have been resolved by the customers themselves.

- *Integration*

  The most effective knowledge management systems are capable not only of resolving customer inquiries and complaints, but also of automatically gathering data which can later result in useful management reports, assisting in root cause analysis, helping agents by automatically updating customer records, and even generating electronic information to be faxed or e-mailed to the customer. Deploying knowledge management systems as "stand alone" entities is counter-productive and one of the most detrimental, yet common, system deployment decisions found in contact center environments today.

- *Relevance*

  If a user has to spent time sifting through the results of a search in order to determine which, if any, information retrieved is relevant to a particular inquiry or complaint, then may be indicative of a poorly designed database or inadequate user interface. Knowledge management systems may employ a variety of search mechanisms or "engines" in an effort to facilitate a relevant response.

Effectiveness

* *Clarity*

  Once relevant information has been retrieved, it is critical that the user can quickly assimilate the contents (and, in the case of a contact center agent, convey the information in real time to the customer). This requires not only outstanding communications skills, but also a significant amount of planning and maintenance on the part of the designer.

* *Integrity*

  Completeness and *accuracy* are the two components of integrity. It is reasonable to assume that when a knowledge management system is first deployed, it will not contain the answer to every customer inquiry or problem, and those that it does address may not always be accurate. Rapid turnaround on incomplete, erroneous or previously non-existent information should therefore be the goal of anyone assigned to *maintain* the integrity of the knowledge base.

In concert, therefore, a strong management focus on collaborative process, technology and content provisioning can pave the way for outstanding customer interaction. Continuous process improvement, integrated system design and vigorously maintained content results in greater customer loyalty and retention. For senior management, however, it must also result in the opportunity to gather meaningful market intelligence, in order that the company can continue to make customer-focused product and service decisions.

Relevant Questions

Question
Do the contact center's information sources take into consideration the unique capabilities and history of the agents?
What is the current process for managing knowledge? Who is responsible for this process?
How much does the contact center rely on tacit knowledge in dealing with customer contacts?*.
How much of the knowledge used by agents is embedded within the enterprise core competencies, mission, values, culture, relationships, policies, procedures, strategy, plans, patents, formulae, brands, methods, structure, workflow and intellectual property?
How much explicit or "hard" knowledge that exists in patents, formulae, copyrights, brands, research reports, databases and best practices is utilized in day-to-day center operations?
How much knowledge that originates outside the contact center (e.g., Internet research) is used by agents?
How much implicit knowledge that exists in enterprise applications, procedural workflow, organizational culture and other implicit processes that manage the company operations on a daily basis is used by contact center agents?

Tacit knowledge resides in the minds of individuals and cannot always be articulated

QA

Quality Assurance

Considerations

A key question in any assessment is whether or not quality assurance evaluations provide the information needed to coach and develop agents to not only provide courteous customer service, but also to actually help to resolve customer issues. Many QA evaluations focus largely on whether or not the agent followed protocol and addressed the customer in a specific manner. This often results in agents receiving similar QA scores for interactions that may have had completely different outcomes from a customer satisfaction perspective.

The key to the successful maintenance of online information and channeling of market intelligence is encompassed by the quality assurance process. This process can span oversight of several tasks, including training, knowledge engineering, systems implementation and maintenance, customer satisfaction evaluation, root cause analysis, and customer contact categorization.

Depending on the prominence management attributes to quality assurance, a cross-functional team may review daily customer contact reports and pending trouble tickets, in addition to gathering and analyzing feedback from agents and managers. The core team should include part-time representatives from training, knowledge engineering, documentation and the development organization, in addition to an expert agent and a front-line agent representative.

The goals of the team, which may also include special projects, could be stated as follows:

- Increase the number of problems and inquiries *resolved at the first point of contact* by empowering both customers and agents with accessible, accurate, understandable and complete online information
- Reduce *contact time* by improving both the speed of response and ease of use through continuous process improvement, efficient database access, and intuitive user interface design
- Establish robust *market intelligence* and *product or service feedback* loops throughout the organization.

Specific Goals:

- Determine missing or inaccurate online policies and procedures, user instructions, troubleshooting scenarios, contact categories and other information which may be relevant to customer contacts
- Assist process owners in identifying inefficient online system processes and suggest improvements by means of system change requests and cost/benefit analysis
- Facilitate root cause analysis of customer contacts for management reporting purposes
- Assist in the analysis and integration of customer satisfaction survey results.

For assessment purposes, the question is how many of the following customer service tasks, if not already considered, can be significantly enhanced by the QA function?

Task	Output
Training	Curriculum improvement and individual agent retraining
Knowledge Engineering	Revised troubleshooting scenarios and links to documentation
Documentation	Revised policies and procedures, user instructions, and other information

Task	Output
Systems Development	System change request and cost/benefit analysis results
Customer Satisfaction	Analysis and integration of survey results
Root Cause Analysis	Management feedback on contact reasons and customer suggestions
Contact Categorization	Updated contact categories based on frequency of occurrence

Table 2 - Potential QA Tasks

The following questions should provide a complete picture of the quality assurance situation at the contact center.

Relevant Questions

Question
Are agents monitored for call quality?
If so: Who performs the monitoring (separate monitoring/quality assurance group, supervisors, other representatives)
Which of the following components of call quality are tracked (accuracy, consistency, tone, in depth knowledge, communication skills, compliance, other)?
How often is an agent monitored?
Does the contact center use a quality assurance tracking application? If so, how satisfactory is its performance?
Do you feel that the purpose and intent of the quality assurance function is clear to contact center agents?
Does the QA function focus primarily on the customer interaction, productivity, or the problem-solving process?
Does QA evaluation classify contacts by type of transaction?
What incentives, if any, are offered to agents who exceed quality assurance standards?
What sort of training is provided to agents regarding the quality assurance initiative?
Is the contact center's social media plan part of the quality improvement initiative?
Is QA feedback used for coaching purposes? If so, how is this conveyed?

Question
Are IT fully engaged in the quality assurance initiative from the perspective of maintenance, upgrades, business rules and report generation?
Is the QA process having the desired effect on center effectiveness?
Does the center employ guidelines for consistent application of quality assurance expectations?
Does the quality monitoring program include the work that agents perform on the computer as well as on the phone with customers?
What specific performance goals are agents focused on in order to positively impact quality assurance measurements?
Do you believe that quality assurance personnel are all scoring agents in a consistent manner?
Are agents encouraged or required to conduct self-evaluation when it comes to quality assurance?
Do managers ever monitor the same contacts as quality assurance personnel and compare marks and notes for consistency?
Who defined the quality objectives for the contact center? What specific considerations were used in defining these objectives?
Do you feel that the contact center's quality assurance objectives are realistic, achievable, timely and easily measurable?
Does the contact center use any existing benchmarks or collaborate with other centers regarding quality assurance?
Does the contact center quality assurance initiative include input from external or allied sources, such as sales and marketing? If so, what are the objectives of those inputs?
How often is the quality assurance program assessed for compliance with overall business goals?
Does the quality assurance initiative provide input to contact center process improvement plans?
Do you believe that some of the quality assurance steps that must be followed by agents are unnecessarily adding to overall talk time and/or after call work time? If so, which ones?
Is company branding, up-selling or cross-selling an integral part of your quality assurance program?
Does the QA process differentiate between senior and inexperienced agents (e.g., senior agents' staff an escalation desk for more difficult customer calls and/or are evaluated for leadership qualities)?
Are there any other types of agent segmentation practiced at the contact center that may impact quality assurance (e.g., specialist

Question
positions)
Do agents undergo any types of certification or additional training that may be considered by quality assurance advocates?
What is the employee attitude towards contact monitoring? How does this affect agent behavior, if at all?
How do you qualitatively assess agents? Is this working adequately or would you like to see it done differently?
What is the total QA monitoring time conducted each day at the contact center? How does this translate to individual agent monitoring time?
Are agents measured for process adherence (e.g., quality monitoring, metrics)? If so, what sort of re-training exists?

Capability

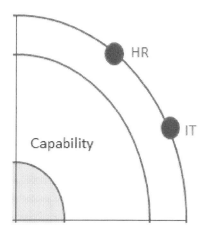

Capability in the context of a contact center assessment is defined as the factors that influence the current and future effectiveness and efficiency of the center. In the contemporary environment, this often translates to technological and analytical capability in terms of cost reduction, business intelligence and customer relationship management systems, as well as human resource considerations.

HR

Human Resources

Considerations

When evaluating effectiveness at a contact center from a human resource perspective, one assessment approach is to conduct a time study using a cross-section of inexperienced and expert agents and managers in order to reveal potential opportunities for improvement. This is closely allied to the workforce management concerns addressed in the efficiency section.

Time study data can be used to:

- Identify inefficiencies in high volume transactional activities
- Refocus resources on specific high-value added activities
- Minimize the future impact of contact volume peaks and valleys.

Ultimately, the goals of the time study will be to eliminate unnecessary work, optimize the sequence of tasks, and help contact center management to realize significant productivity gains across the entire operation.

Each task identified during the time study should be considered based on the following:

1. Frequency of performance
2. Time spent
3. Criticality/significance of error
4. Task necessity

Capability

5. Impact of task performance on job success.

Once the goal of the time study has been determined, the overall framework must be defined. In order to be successful, a time study must:

- Have a management commitment to act on the findings
- Have a clearly defined project scope and timeline
- Be clearly aligned with ongoing productivity initiatives
- Provide intuitive mechanisms for data gathering
- Encourage proactive task-owner and participant feedback
- Make results transparent to the entire organization

Here are some typical focal points that the time study may highlight for consideration:

- Which contact center tasks involve the highest-volume and/or most routine transactions?
- What sub tasks are relevant to each?
- How are these sub-tasks ideally handled or delegated?
- What type of work do these sub tasks involve (e.g., inbound calls, outbound emails, documentation, system inputs, etc.)?
- How much time does each task typically take?
- When do these tasks occur in the context of day-to-day operations?
- Which of these tasks are considered to be 'specialized'?
- What are the opportunities for cross-organizational training?

Apart from the data gathered by contact center routing systems, an internal record of operational tasks usually exists in some consolidated format, typically in a time tracking system. The question is whether the data collected can generate a blueprint of contact center activity and opportunities for improvement.

Preparing for and conducting an Assessment Time Study

Apart from the critical need for senior management support, there are three practical components involved in preparing for and conducting a time study. These are:

- Task Categorization
- Data Gathering
- Analysis and reporting

Task Categorization

From a tactical perspective, an initial exercise is to create or verify a list of all of the tasks for which the contact center is responsible, and to make sure that this is categorized and ordered in an intuitive manner. There are dozens of tasks and potentially *hundreds* of sub tasks carried out on a daily basis in a typical contact center. For the purposes of a time study, the key is to group these tasks into meaningful categories that allow participants to quickly find the 'bucket' into which any particular task that they perform belongs.

It may be determined that it is possible to capture 90% of all tasks at the highest level using around a dozen categories. Given that certain categories do not apply to particular areas of responsibility, it is feasible (and desirable, depending on the tool used for data gathering) to cull the list even further based on the targeted user population.

The importance of the high-level categorization of work cannot be overemphasized in the context of a time study. While it is important to include 'catch-all' categories, such as 'Administration', if as a result of poor study design participants classify 50% of their work in this category, and of these classifications 25% of the accompanying task descriptions are abstract or indecipherable, then the accuracy of the results is significantly compromised.

The time study must also capture information about the number of task transactions that occur within a particular period of time, as well as a free-form text field for descriptions of any task that does not easily translate to the pre-defined listings. Given that a decision is made to attribute only functional or group manager names to each task logged, rather than individuals, this capability also needs to be built into the study framework.

Data Gathering Approach

While it is feasible to conduct a time study using only a pencil and paper to gather information, to facilitate analysis it is recommended that an application with the capacity to aggregate and sort data, which is universally available by all resources within the operations group, should be utilized. Using intuitive and common conventions such as single selection drop down lists wherever possible enables participants to rapidly log data. The fewer onuses that are put on the user to physically enter information, the better. Pre-defined lists are a necessity in this regard. Given that due diligence to task and sub task definitions has occurred, there is no reason why participants should not be able to locate a pre-existing description of the work accomplished. A facility for users to provide proactive feedback on perceived opportunities for improvement and apparent issues with the data gathering tool is particularly important at the onset of the time study.

Rapid assessment and dissemination of feedback from the first day's data capture is critical to the ultimate usability of data from the study. In this respect, the time study analyst should immediately look for anomalies, not for trends. The first two days of the time study can be used to refine the design of the data collection medium in the event that there are obvious omissions or flaws that are causing confusion, invalid or incomplete data entry, or unnecessary delays for the user population.

The data gathering tool should list only those elements that are considered critical to maintaining the overall integrity of the time study. These might include date, duration, count, category, task, sub task, action, description, and department, group or individual name (if the decision is made to attribute tasks to individuals). The tool should not allow participants to create their own categories, tasks, etc.

Very often, it is found that anomalies are occurring either because (a) the tasks defined in the Time Study from the outset were inadequate or (b) participants were unable to interpret the available selections, or because the selections did not make sense to the participant in the context of the work accomplished. However, even after exhaustive research, it may be found that a significant percentage of tasks simply do not fit into the study parameters. As will be shown in the discussion of analytics, this introduces a significant finding that must be emphasized in the results.

Each participant must be trained on how to use the time study data capture tool. This can be achieved by first having the analyst describe to the responsible managers and the study coordinator exactly what approach will be taken and what outcomes are anticipated from the study data. The analyst should describe what is considered acceptable data and what is not. For example, if the goal of the study is purely to measure work (e.g., the statistical analysis of durations involving a certain task), then it should be made clear that the main goal is for the participant to capture the exact task and the number of task repetitions, if any, for a specific period of time. It should also be emphasized that data pertaining to non-work related activities that occur during normal hours of operation are irrelevant in this context.

It must be definitively established when the time study will begin and how long it will last. Time frames for the duration of study tasks are also important. The goal is not to be intrusive, but to allow participants to capture the context of their everyday work in manageable segments. It may be decided that 15 minute intervals are the minimum time frames for usable data capture – any less is overkill, anything more may be considered too broad.

Given that the intent of the study is not to focus on individual performance, but rather to understand the distribution and execution of work across functions, it is important from the outset to clearly state and continually emphasize study guidelines in order to maximize the quality of the data collected.

Capability

Analysis and Reporting

As with any data gathering initiative, measurement is an intrinsic part of the perceived success or failure of the time study. Efforts to gather, analyze and synthesize study information require the assignment of numbers to tasks. This can be achieved through the use of common statistical tools such as mean, median and standard deviation. However, conviction that the results of the time study are usable requires substantive proof involving two considerations – those of *reliability* and *validity*.

In short, reliability concerns the consistency of measurement. <u>In other words, when the same task is measured twice, does it realize the same result</u>? As an example, did the same individual or group performing the same task on more than one occasion achieve results that were consistent with one another? Reliability may prove to be a somewhat cryptic in a time study that measures time spent in, for example, fifteen minute intervals. This is where decisions will be made on the use of particular statistical tools in order to draw overall conclusions.

The second key measurement – validity – involves the usage of data that proves that <u>the task being analyzed is significantly correlated with important elements of job performance</u>. Validity may be measured from several perspectives involving more or less complex arguments, but the ultimate goal is to be able to show that any conclusions drawn from the time study data are based on the existence of solid supporting data. As one example, using the data collected, can a *conclusion* be effectively reached that a particular task is taking far more resource time than it should, based on its relative impact upon the overall productivity of the clinical operations environment?

Unless there is such conclusive evidence of the need for change, whether in terms of task assignment, training, resource allocation, technology support, or other area of concern, the influence of the time study results may otherwise be limited to an interesting fact-finding exercise that provides insights into activities whose characteristics might otherwise have remained common misconceptions, such as the amount of resource time allocated to trials in the month prior to first patient visit, or the resource drain caused by a single trial audit, or the percentage of time spent in meetings or writing emails, and so on.

The use of basic statistical measures, such as mean, median, and standard deviation will not only augment the reliability and validity of study data, but will also typically reveal some 'quick wins' in terms of work measures for particular tasks. For example, if the overall mean (or average time) for a single repetition of a relatively high volume task is x minutes, and the median (which attributes less importance to outlier results) time is y minutes, with a major time differential between the two measures, the results suggest that there are significant inconsistencies in task execution that may be caused by a particular group or subset of users. Similarly, if the standard deviation from the mean is extraordinarily high, it may be found that – for example - training on a complex task is urgently required.

Apart from the anticipated large volume of administrative work, one obvious point of comparison would be the average number of hours worked each week by group, together with a statistical correlation to the average amount of time per task by group. It may be found that groups with the highest number of working hours also spend the most time conducting administrative tasks. In the case of managers and specialists, further discovery of the reasons why such work is not being delegated may include a plethora of revealing responses, including a lack of confidence in understudies, perceived lack of time to train others, or a perception that everyone else is too busy to take on more work, etc.

Five importance task differentiators were outlined earlier - frequency of performance, time spent, criticality/significance of error, task necessity and the impact of task performance on job success. By assigning these properties to the time study results, a classification of relative task influence can be built. This ranking of tasks can be achieved by a combination of study results and management consensus, and will be critical when considering reliability, validity, and focal points when the study results and recommendations are finalized.

Pinpointing tasks that offer opportunities for improvement is a key to fulfilling the goal of the study, i.e., finding ways to increase productivity.

For example, any work described as an 'informal meeting' should immediately be questioned. It also stands to reason that managers and specialists should not typically be engaged in data collection, report drafting, filing, copying, data entry, or conversely for tasks for which the individual concerned has no qualification, or tasks which are undertaken by a manager simply 'because I like doing that and/or 'I'm good at that and it's fun'.

Other 'low-hanging fruit' are those opportunities for improvement or anomalies that demand immediate attention and correction, such as tasks that no one can easily fit into any category that was defined as within the scope of operational responsibilities from the outset. This situation suggests that, perhaps without management approval, resources are being utilized to perform tasks that sit outside the realm of operations as this is defined within that particular clinical setting. The typical explanation in such cases ranges from: "I never knew we were spending so much time doing work that really belongs in the field" or "this is unexpected rework due to issues beyond my jurisdiction".

Typical Broad-based Time Study Findings:

- Too much time is being spent on tasks of questionable value in terms of overall contact center goals
- Disparate customer contact/management and support initiatives are causing excessive task redundancy
- Processing of tasks that are inappropriate for centralized operations is blurring work boundaries and resulting in unofficial 'dotted-line' work silos
- Particular functions are demanding too much local knowledge to be effectively centralized.

Despite the initial interest generated by the high-level discoveries, such as 'the outdated system support infrastructure is resulting in excessive and unnecessary manual work', unless there is a specific plan of action based on findings, the ultimate takeaway will be "So what? Now you know what we have to put up with every day!" Any analyst presenting the details study data must be cognizant of the relationship between his or her findings and the strategic direction of upper management.

Using the data to examine resource utilization within operational sub-groups is an obvious output of the time study. If an organization employs a dedicated group of individuals to handle archiving, for example, then it stands to reason that the results emanating from this team will predominantly involve some form of document handling. However, it may be found that despite the best efforts of the manager to define logical tasks executed by the group in the time study selections, that a certain percentage of the time participants were unable to correlate their work with those expectations.

Considering study results from 'rolled-up' perspectives is particularly important. For example, if data shows that tasks of a certain complexity merit additional resource allocation, then this is data that should impact the study recommendations. Similarly, if results show that tasks that do not involve specialized knowledge are predominant, then this information must be utilized to drive productivity improvements through more efficient resource sharing. Perhaps the recommendation here will involve structural change, such as the grouping of certain contact center resources into a single 'tier'.

While many study findings can be indicative of significant opportunities for improvement from a resource productivity perspective, there are inevitably indicators of bottlenecks and other process-related issues that demand attention.

Given that the study has enabled senior management to identify and address misplaced, inappropriate, and inefficient areas of work, thereby freeing up a certain amount of available resource time, then the time study has highlighted the opportunity to engage those resources in work that realizes critical gains in customer satisfaction, quality, and process improvement.

Capability

Supervisor Activity (example)

Activity	Cumulative Elapsed Time
Previous day's statistics to team (TM)	
Team member –where to find information (AC)	
Assist call - team member needs service recovery (CA)	
Begins work on completing service recovery database (OA)	
Assist call - team member needs quote approval (CA)	
Reviews schedule and break requests (TM)	
Reviews Call Management System (TP)	
Begins weekly team performance charts (OA)	
Assist call from another team member (AC)	
Distribute faxes (TM)	
Team member question (AC)	
Continues weekly team performance charts (OA)	
Call from account manager requesting an escalation (RM)	
Returns to weekly performance charts (OA)	
Reviews CMS data (TP)	
Assist call from team member (AC)	
Customer assist call from another team member (CA)	
Sends data to process improvement team by e-mail (OA)	

Activity	Cumulative Elapsed Time
Completes weekly performance charts (OA)	
Call from CMS monitor about agent with high talk time (TP)	
Listens to agents taking calls (TD)	
Assist call from team member - irate customer (CA)	
Calls agent back with feedback from customer call (TD)	
Makes entry in CRM database (OA)	
Call from account manager looking for a report (RM)	
Works on report (RM)	
Team member question (AC)	
Quality analyst drops delivers evaluation sheets (TM)	
Checks for any agent issues/feedback (TD)	
Completes report for account manager (RM)	

Table 3 - Contact Center Supervisors – A Composite View

Description of Table: This table represents a composite view of a certain time period in a contact center manager's day.

Elapsed time: This is the time from the beginning of a day (time 0) to the time that a particular activity is *completed*. For example, the activity "receives call from account manager looking for a report" completes 350 minutes after the beginning of the day. By this time, the agent has completed talking to the account manager. For each activity, the difference between the cumulative elapsed time associated with the activity and the cumulative elapsed time associated with the previous activity gives the duration of the activity. For example, the agent talked to the account manager for (350-345) = 5 minutes

TM represents team management activities. These represent activities that need to be done to manage the group as a whole. Example are updating payroll, verifying absences, sending out team messages, team meetings etc.

OA represents documentation/reporting/organizational activities. These are the activities that are needed to inform the organization about specific customer problems or issues, or reporting on performance. For example, talking to account managers about specific customer problems or issues, sending e-mail to account managers are typically these kinds of activities. These activities also include special projects, staff meetings etc.

AC represents an assist call for information.

CA represents customer assistance in dealing with an issue, or to make decisions regarding service.

RM represents relationship management activities. These are the activities required to maintain and support relationships with the field, including talking to account managers and responding to their requests

TP represents team productivity monitoring activities. These are the activities related to monitoring of CMS, and checking up on agents in ACD, ACW or AUX modes for too long

TD represents team development activities. These include call monitoring, walking the floor and coaching activities.

Activity Summary: The following should be used to describe an activity summary for a typical day

ACTIVITY	TIME SPENT	% TOTAL TIME
Team Management		
Status/Documentation/ Organizational		
Customer related assist calls		
Information related assist calls		
Customer Relationship Management		
Team Productivity Monitoring		
Team Development Activities		

Analysis of activities: The activity summary table is intended to show how the manager's time is distributed among many different activities, requiring constant juggling of responsibilities. Each set of activities may require the manager to assume a different role. From an efficiency perspective, the question is whether or not the manager is engaged in tasks that (a) could reasonably be allocated to a centralized group, such as quality control (b) should always be handled by the front lines, but are not due to training shortfalls or (c) add to the efficient management of the contact center.

Contact Center Agents – A Composite View

A chronological view of front line agent tasks is useful in identifying inefficiencies pertaining to work performed outside of direct customer contact. The most obvious example is when an agent enters the after call work state in order to perform a routine, non-emergent task while customer calls are in queue.

Activity	ACD State	Elapsed Time
Send Fax	AUX	396 seconds
Takes customer call	ACD	120 seconds
Writes comments	ACW	97 seconds
Calls Sales Representative	AUX OUT	254 seconds
Reads Email	ACW	96 seconds
Takes customer call	ACD	345 seconds
Writes comments	ACW	113 seconds
Checks Voice Mail	ACW	89 seconds
Requests Manager help	AUX	210 seconds
Responds to chat request	ACD	632 seconds
Writes comments	ACW	76 seconds
Calls field rep	AUX OUT	478 seconds
Creates customer record	ACW	198 seconds

Table 4 - Contact Center Agents – A Composite View

By repeating these observations among a cross-section of new and experienced agents, the cumulative data may be used to identify inefficiencies that lead to longer hold times for customers and ineffective usage of agent and manager time.

One underlying question in any contact center that experiences high rates of after call work is whether any ACW tasks may be batched or deferred to set periods of 'closed key time'.

Relevant Questions

Question
What is the current career pathing within the Contact Center (internal / external promotions)?
How are employees motivated (incentives, time off with pay, financial rewards, and/or seniority incentives)?

Question
Do you conduct employee surveys to judge motivation, morale, and/or customer service and customer satisfaction issues)?
What is the number of days per year allocated to training staff? Why?
Have you identified the agents best suited to social media, web chat and other non-call activities?
How are training requirements determined (formal curriculum, customer satisfaction surveys, employee requests, management objectives, professional development plan, and/or skills assessment)?
What is the customer service representative turnover rate at the Contact Center? Why do you think it is so high/low?
What is the supervisor/manager turnover rate at the Contact Center? Why is it so high/low?
Does the contact center maintain a database of agent skills?
How is training for new technologies conducted (via classroom, CDs, video, side by side sessions, etc.)?
How could your training facilities be improved?
What are the things you enjoy least about working at the center?
What are the top causes of stress at the center (e.g., management, irate callers, call volumes, queues, job security, monitoring, paper work, inflexibility, lack of training, personnel issues, team structures)?
How would you rate the morale of the center?
How do you rate your opportunities for advancement within the center?
How would you rate your opportunities for advancement elsewhere in the organization?
How would you rate your initial training? How could it be improved?
How would you rate the ongoing (day-to-day) training you receive?
What would you like additional training in (time management, IT, service, policy, management, products)?
How would you rate incentives at the contact center?
What do the reps you supervise think of the employee recognition and incentive plans?
What is the most important training that you provide to your reps?

Capability

Question
How do reps react to monitoring and subsequent feedback?
How can you improve the center as a supervisor?
How would you rate morale at the center?
How are training requirements determined (satisfaction surveys, employee requests, management objectives, development plan, skills assessment, etc.)?
Describe the steps that you go through to perform your work
Have you changed some activities to meet WFM needs?
What impact has it had on your work activities?
What are the places that rework occurs?
How do you handle rework?
What are reasons for rework?
What fraction of orders get reworked?
What fraction of activity time does rework take?
What prevents you from doing it right the first time?
How do you prioritize your work?
How do you decide between incoming and existing work?
How do you clear backlogs?
Do you always go by the schedule?
What are the key reasons for delays in the process?
How do you deal with delays?
What do you do when an activity is behind schedule?
How do you think you can improve the process?
What are the things that will help you do your work better?
Does the work change as you get more experience?
Do you use Policies and Procedures?
Do you use a knowledge management system?
How different is what you actually do from the current standard operating procedures?
Does your activity take the same time for all orders?
What contributes to the variability of activity times?
How is work assigned to you?
What do you do if you have too much work?
Do you distribute the work to someone else?
What entities do you have to interface with in your work?
How do you handle these interfaces?
How do you escalate your work if there are issues?
Are there situations where more than one person is needed?

IT ●

Information Technology

Considerations

When it comes to the crucial area of information technology support in a contact center, the assessor should ask the obvious questions first:

- Uninterrupted availability of the network?
- The Interactive Voice Response (IVR) unit is always functional?
- The Automatic Call Distributor (ACD) is configured correctly?
- Computer-Telephony Integration (CTI) functions are available?
- The contact management system is always appropriately managed?
- The WFM system is adequately facilitating all incoming contacts?
- The agent's desktop system is always functional?

Does the contact center IT framework include the following?

- Multi-channel (i.e., telephone, e-mail, chat, web callback, web call-through, collaboration, fax, and mail) contact tracking and chronological client contact history, integrated with an order management module.

- Functionality that enables sales, service, marketing and other client-facing groups to share chronological client contact histories, thereby ensuring a unified client view regardless of the contact media or purpose of the contact. This is a core business driver of CRM.

- Workflow management (including client commitments, case and sub-case structures, real-time internal notifications and exception reports, and business rules to include escalation paths, order tracking status checks, client event notifications, etc.).

- Ability to ensure that any particular customer requirement (i.e., a unique 'case') is tracked to completion, even if that case involves several different groups within the organization.

- Computer-Telephony Integration (CTI) and potential communications server (i.e., Internet, e-mail, fax, and telephone) integration, including real-time record transferal and skills-based routing components. This option requires CTI 'hooks' in an application and would rarely be applied to a home-grown solution.

  CTI is a potentially powerful "add-on" to a CRM solution. Careful analysis is required in order to ensure that the cost of CTI implementation can tangibly contribute to bottom line cost efficiencies.

- Integrated Knowledge Management (including automatically triggered SOP retrieval based on selection of a particular contact type, knowledge-based systems linkage, online scripting, and computer-based training modules)

  Many CRM applications have successfully integrated knowledge management systems in order to facilitate the rapid resolution of a particular customer problem. Again, this level of integration is geared towards ensuring accurate "on-the-fly" customer communications.

Which of the following does the contact center IT environment support?

- Retrieval of Customer Transaction History
- Contact Categorizations
- Disposition of Sales Leads to the Field
- Integration with Knowledge Management systems
- Advanced CTI integration
- Creation of User Privilege Classes

- Business Rules for Escalations & Complaints
- Proactive Callback Commitment Tracking
- Customer Value Indicators
- Online scripting
- Online voice of the customer
- Management Reporting Facilities.

Are all of the following situations transparent to the agent?

Enhancement	Scenarios
Retrieval of multi-channel customer transaction history	- Customer is a high value repeat caller - Customer has spent several minutes attempting to use the IVR - Customer refers to previous call, chat session, social media, e-mail, fax or postal mail contact - Customer calls back several times regarding an order - Customer is using the web site and has an inquiry or problem - Customer has spoken to agent previously (customer relationship management)

Relevant Questions

Question
What equipment is used to service the contact center (PBX, IVR, ACD, CTI, Workstations, Headsets, Predictive Dialers)
Who provides and maintains this equipment?
What disaster recovery contingencies are in place for this center?
How is the network configured (T1s, DID, Work at Home, Tie Lines, ISDN, CO)?
What service level agreements exist between IT and the contact center?
What are your 800 number costs (calls v. minutes, usage charges)
What software is used (CMS, Contact Management, Enterprise Resources, Sales Force Automation, Legacy, Voice Mail, E-Mail, Fax, Management Reporting)
Upgrade plans for the coming months (voice recognition, enterprise systems, hardware upgrades, etc.)?
Who is responsible for scripting and maintaining the IVR? What kind

Question
of user needs analysis was performed?
Is there any coordination between the web site functionality and the IVR functions?
ANI or CTI? If CTI, how effective is it in this environment (i.e., hit rate/response time)?
How many fields are populated automatically via CTI? % of hits anticipated in the future?
When the caller transfers out of the IVR to an agent, does the agent see any record of transactions within the IVR?
What improvements would you like to see made in the current configuration? Why?
What is your system design methodology - rapid prototyping, task analysis, etc.?
What is the change request process at the contact center?
What sort of systems integration issues exist? Can these be resolved?
Do you use a faxback system? If so, how often is it used?
Can users chat, monitor online forums and send faxes from their desks?
When an agent transfers a call, do any data screens also get transferred?
Which factors impact how a contact will be routed (network routing based on geography, time of day, agent availability, queue lengths at centers)?
Total contacts to all centers v. average % of contacts to this center? (if applicable)
What sort of Information Technology initiatives would you like to see occur?
Do you feel that the IVR function is viable or should it be eliminated? Why?
What do you think of your IT support framework in general? How could it be improved?
How would you rate the desktop systems that you work with at the contact center?
Technology Perspective - planned improvements?
Which organization is responsible for maintaining the web site and knowledge bases?
What efforts are being made to create cohesive multi-channel customer service (i.e., integrated technology solutions)?

IVR

How many of these Best Practices are supported?

Opportunity	Value	Benchmark
Increase IVR Usage/ Facilitate Initial Call Handling		<ul><li>Automate routine calls</li><li>Optimize key response feature</li><li>Conduct human factors usability assessment</li><li>Facilitate user interaction via voice recognition</li><li>Use "double zero" prompt strategy</li><li>Proactively provide advance keying directions</li><li>Increase queue time</li><li>Provide approximate queue times</li><li>Pre-record agent greeting</li><li>Integrate IVR usage with ANI / CTI</li><li>Conduct IVR usability testing</li><li>Analyze and record ROFC per customer</li><li>Implement web-enabled IVR</li></ul>

How many of the following benchmarks for Caller Menus and IVRs are supported?

1. Order options by usage frequency
2. Use no more than 3-4 menu choices
3. Use short and succinct options
4. Always state "what" before "how"
5. Do not aggregate options under one menu choice
6. Permit advance keying
7. Warn users of information required in advance
8. Use typical customer nomenclature
9. Evaluate scripts for sentence structure and grade level
10. Ensure key response is sensitive
11. Permit zero out at any time.

CRM System

Which of the following attributes are supported by the current CRM system?

Opportunity	ROI/Value	Benchmark
Facilitate contact tracking for management reporting and customer relationship purposes		▪ Assess customer transaction values v. cost v. longevity ▪ Alert field/inside sales staff of customer activities ▪ Periodic management reports of contact volumes by call type and media (web, fax, e-mail, phone, IVR) ▪ Use historical customer contact data to proactively sell value-added services to appropriate customers ▪ Integrate CTI with IVR activities for automatic transaction logging ▪ Automate time-stamped notations based on other system interactions, such as billing adjustments ▪ Social media monitoring ▪ Proactively notify agents of callback commitments ▪ Apply business rules to ensure that all open contacts are handled appropriately or escalated ▪ Automatically organize social conversations into queues based on content ▪ View conversations from multiple social sources ▪ Route social conversations to agents based on business rules ▪ Mine social conversations ▪ Outgoing social responses adhere to corporate SOPs.

Attribute	System 1	System 2
Cost per agent		
Licensing Cost (Year One)		
Licensing (> Year One)		
Training Costs		
Annual Licenses		
CTI Integration		
Commitment Tracking		
User Privilege Class		
Online Decision Support		
Online scripting		
Online customer surveys		
Customer Value Indicators		
Link Types to Help		
Mobile Computing		
Call Tracking		
Multi-channel Tracking		
Online Documentation		
Network Computing		
Notification		
Business Rules		
Internet		
Ongoing Support		
Quality Updates		
Process Flow		
Sales Force Automation		
Live chat		
Redirect rate		
Quality of response		
Transfer rate		
First post resolution		

Table 5 - Example of an IT Evaluation of CRM System

Knowledge Management System

Example of Contact Center Business Process/Requirements

1. **Initiate a knowledge management QIT**

   A critical success factor in maintaining any knowledge management
   system is the ability to rectify omissions, inaccuracies, accessibility
   issues, and ambivalent content as quickly as possible. Agents should
   never access the same piece of incorrect data twice in a week, or
   twice fail to find a certain node of information because the jargon used
   was not considered pertinent, etc. Keeping up to date with online
   knowledge is the only way any such system can succeed. This
   requires process development, the initiation of a QIT involving
   training, rotational agents, supervisors, and the knowledge
   management team.

2. **Build an Intranet**

   An Intranet would allow the knowledge engineer(s) to dynamically
   update erroneous, outdated, unclear, or incomplete information
   rapidly, without any need for compilation of code. It would also allow
   the web designer/human factors engineer to prototypically adjust
   graphical screen designs based on usability testing/task analysis.
   Also, the availability of powerful hypertext capabilities will allow the
   knowledge engineer(s) to create intuitive linkages between disparate
   nodes of text and graphics.

   The object of any knowledge management system must be to enable
   users to rapidly access relevant information. This is especially true in
   call center environments, where inexperienced agents can benefit
   enormously from "real time" information presented during the course
   of a call. The best knowledge management systems are the ones that
   actually assist the agent in providing outstanding and compliant
   customer service.

3. **Implement a robust search engine for ease of access**

The biggest potential flaw of any knowledge management system is a search engine that fails to match a user request appropriately. This is the single biggest reason for agents "giving up" on even the most elaborate systems. The knowledge acquisition team must make every effort to identify jargon, special terminology, and cryptic search terminology that users might use to find a particular piece of information. This requires detailed usability testing and analysis of the content.

Also, finding a host of "matches" that appear to have little or nothing to do with the search term used is almost as bad as finding no matches at all. This often results from the use of inferior search engines or poorly designed knowledge. The best contact center Intranets include a highly robust search facility.

4. **Link relevant nodes of information to the contact management system for seamless interaction where possible**

Some contact tracking systems assist agents by automatically linking to a relevant node of information in the knowledge management system based on agent selection of contact type and detail. In other words, if the contact type is *Billing*, and the detail is *Invoice Dispute*, the system will open the pertinent Intranet link to the policies and procedures relevant to that contact type.

5. **Mirror non-proprietary content with the Internet site**

It is important that content development pertinent to customer service on the Internet web site mirrors that which is used to populate the proposed contact center Intranet. This way, center management can be certain that the customer is receiving consistent information regarding service offerings from the company.

6. **Integrate Intranet access with the contact management system's auto-notations**

   Sophisticated contact tracking systems allow users to auto-notate a customer contact record by selecting a particular text node in the knowledge management system (i.e., a key indicator of the resolution for a particular contact).

7. **Conduct a cost-benefit analysis pertinent to the use of troubleshooting application**

   Many contact centers use troubleshooting systems in order to enable agents to problem-solve customer issues. Typically, these systems are most effective in product support environments, where the customer is experiencing particular difficulty in configuring or operating the product. Using natural language, keyword, or Boolean logic, the system responds to user input with a series of questions that are used to reach a pre-defined level of probability, at which point the user will suggest the resolution to the customer.

8. **Build a business case for mandatory usage of the knowledge management system for certain contact types.**

   The decision as to whether or not to mandate access to a knowledge management system for certain contact types is typically controversial. Many senior agents resist any such mandate, simply because they feel that there is nothing that they do not know regarding customer contacts. However, impromptu contact observations often demonstrate significant differences in interpreting policies and procedures, even amongst the most senior agents.

   Knowledge management systems sometimes fail because agents are not proactively engaged in ensuring that the quality and integrity of the knowledge is indisputable. Many systems languish within the first few weeks of deployment, because agents complain that "We can never find what we're looking for". This is not always a search engine issue. It is often because the information simply is not there it was overlooked during the knowledge acquisition stage. The most effective way to engage experienced agents in any knowledge management endeavor, therefore, is to use them as the subject matter experts whose insights will help newer reps deal with customer issues. It is our experience that senior agents take pride in seeing their contributions published to the entire center – in a sense they become the advocates and owners of the system. Financial or other incentives are also used by some contact centers to ensure the integrity of the knowledge management system.

Business Intelligence

The following are some examples of business intelligence reports that may be generated from contact center data:

1. **Missed sales opportunities/account cancellations** (e.g., pre-sales inquiries, customer suggestions, competitive activities, etc.)

2. **Potential product or service improvements** (e.g., troubleshooting and other product or service support contacts)

3. **Potential customer contact improvements** (e.g., telemarketing complaints, missed commitments, social media complaints, queue times, hours of operation, etc.)

4. **Potential Cost-cutting Opportunities** (e.g., elimination of misdirects, repeat calls, lengthy contacts, billing errors, system deficiencies, online information deficits, etc.).

#	Report Content	Business Need	Sub-elements Required	Recipient
1	Pre-sales inquiries which did not result in a sale/post-sale cancellations	Identify the reasons why a customer did not choose/ retain the company's	• Price Issue • Features Required • Branch/ Store Location	Executive Committee

#	Report Content	Business Need	Sub-elements Required	Recipient
		product or service and rectify as necessary	• Credit Rejection • Preliminary Inquiry Only • Other	
2	Business Complaints by Category	Identify areas of customer dissatisfaction and rectify as necessary	• Billing Error Complaints • Marketing complaints • Price Complaint • Quality Complaint	Billing Marketing Product Mngt
3	Customer Care Complaints by category	Identify opportunities for improvement in the call center – customer interface	• Time in queue • IVR • Social Media scripting/functions • Call Center Care Level • Missed commitments	Contact Center Mngt
4	Product/Service Problems by category	Identify opportunities for improvement in the design of products/ services	• Specific problem type • Product/ Service Suggestion	Product Mngt
5	Missing or erroneous online information	Identify any information which is not immediately available to resolve a	• Missing, erroneous or unclear procedures • Missing, erroneous or	Content/ Knowledge Engineers

#	Report Content	Business Need	Sub-elements Required	Recipient
		customer inquiry	unclear troubleshooti ng information	
6	Repeat calls, misdirects & missed commitments	Identify opportunities to reduce costs through the monitoring of unnecessary contacts with the customer care environment	• Agent suggestions • Repeat call tracking • Missed commitment tracking	Contact Center Mngt
7	Billing Inquiries other than complaints	Identify opportunities for improvement within the billing environment	• Bill format • Language facilitation • Rates notification • Special Offer Support	Billing

Report Examples

- **Pre-sales Inquiry**

  Resulted in sale (Yes/No)? No:

  - Price Issue
  - Features Required
  - Branch/Store Location
  - Credit Rejection
  - Preliminary Inquiry Only
  - Other

- **Post-sales Support**

  Product/Service Problem

  - Specific Problem Type

- Product/Service Suggestion

Business Complaint

- Billing Error Complaint
- Marketing Complaint (Direct Mail, Telemarketing, Advertising, etc.)
- Price Complaint
- Quality Complaint

Account Maintenance

- Change Name
- Change Address
- Change Billing Cycle
- Add Feature (specify)

Account Cancellation (explain)

- Did not meet needs (specify)
- Competitive Offer
- Out of business, etc.

Billing Inquiry

- Price Plans
- Special Offers
- Reconciliation.

Differentiation

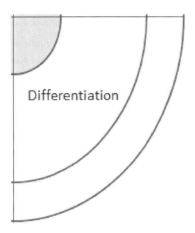

Differentiation

Differentiation in the context of a contact center assessment is defined as identifying opportunities for improvement via understanding of competitive practices.

Relevant Questions

Question
Is the perception that the company provides superior/inferior value to its competition?
Is it the perception that the contact center plays an important/inferior role in influencing customer perceptions of the company?
What impact will improvements in the contact center have on improving customer perceptions of the company's value in general?
What are the most important differentiators that the contact center offers to customers v. the competition?

Simple Benchmarking

Depending on the scope of the assessment, the feasibility of conducting some simple benchmarking could be considered. This would involve creating mock scenarios with questions specifically targeted towards identifying differences between levels of service at both the contact center being assessed and that company's closest competitors. The same questions would be asked in every case and the answers evaluated from the perspective of the following:

Feature	Contact Center	Competitor 1
Timeliness		
Empowerment		
Centralization		
Knowledgeability		
Courtesy		
Responsiveness		
Sales Orientation		
Systems Support		
Clarity		

Table 6 - Contact Center Competitive Differentiation

Value Perspective

Two obvious questions that the assessment must strive to answer are whether or not the contact center (a) adds viable revenue to the company and/or (b) adds value to customers.

The following table represents a possible value analysis of a typical 'cost center' approach to the contact center's core customer service activities:

Core Activity	Adds Revenue	Adds Value
Orders	Yes	No
Billing	No	No
Quotes	No	No
Complaint Handling	No	No

Table 7 - Contact Center Value Perspective

One differentiation output of the traditional contact center assessment, therefore, would be recommendations pertaining to the role of the center as a profit or 'value-added' environment.

Ways in which the typical contact center can change the 'cost center' perspective and differentiate itself from the competition:

- Become the single point of contact for the company's current and future valued-added services
- Provide both regular and customized specialty services directly to the customer
- Participate or assist in sales functions
- Become the primary point of collection and aggregation of customer relationship management-oriented data
- Take the lead in identifying profitable customers and designing targeted new services

- Serve as the pilot center for consolidating social media, ecommerce, web and other customer contact points, as well as testing new customer access technologies.

In order to justify these expenses for repositioning the contact center in the future, the assessment should stress the need to build awareness and credibility within the larger organization. Awareness can be built by recommending a strategic plan for the center that articulates the vision of how the center will evolve and grow over time. Such a plan should be developed in collaboration with senior managers in Marketing, Sales and Operations. Future requests for technology enhancements can then be justified on the basis of the agreed upon plan.

The assessment should also point out that awareness alone is not enough to ensure the competitive advantage of the contact center. The center must build credibility by demonstrating that it is managing current operations in the most efficient and effective manner possible.

The assessment must also underline the need for the center to eliminate wasteful activities without reducing the quality of service provided to customers. Topics such as outsourcing and automation for competitive advantage should be fully explored. Any such recommendation must be accompanied by a disciplined process management and improvement initiative supported by data analysis to ensure that the center is providing the most effective service efficiently. This in turn may free up capacity that can then be used for growing the organization, and will also provide a results based management infrastructure as the contact center also takes on more complex tasks in the future.

Comparative Performance

Using available industry benchmarks, efficiency metrics can also be used as a basis for competitive differentiation, as shown in the example below:

Metric	Contact Center Performance
Cost Per Contact	Lower than industry average
AHT	Higher than industry average
ASA	Best-in-class
ACW	Higher than industry average
Availability	Average

A summary of conclusions might read as follows:

- The contact center performs better than industry benchmarks in terms of cost per call and average speed of answer
- The contact center is average in terms of agent availability
- The contact center performs worse than benchmarks in terms of after call work and average handling time.

Metric	Current	Competitor	Best Practice
ASA	100% in 15 seconds	90% in 20 seconds	100% in 30 seconds
Abandonment	2.3%	< 2% after 10 seconds	< 5%
Occupancy	54-64%	>78%	> 68%
ATT	124 seconds	118 seconds	222 seconds
ACW	58 seconds	< 10 seconds	57 seconds
Availability	9-19%	< 10%	13%
Total Talk %	45-46% of Paid Time	> 65% of Paid Time	>57% of Paid Time

Metric	Current	Competitor	Best Practice
Closed Key Time	No	Yes (15 minutes/day)	Yes (15-30 minutes/day)
Service Level (Av.)	80-90%	>90%	87%
Hold Tracking	No	Yes	Yes
Transfer Tracking	No	Yes	Yes
Inbound/ Outbound Call Ratio	27%	Unknown	NA
ROFC	No	Measured (no metric)	78%
% of Customer Base calling	Unknown	Unknown	13%
Customer Satisfaction	TBD	95%	94%
Customer Loyalty	TBD	Unknown	87%
Customer Segmentation	Platinum	Call Prioritization	NA
CTI	Yes	Yes	Yes
Call Tracking	No	Yes	Yes
Repeat Call Tracking	No	Yes	Yes
Escalation Tracking	Yes	Yes	Yes
Knowledge Management	No	Yes	NA
Service Intranet	No	TBD	NA
Sales Lead Generation	No	Yes	Yes
Cost Per Call	$3.00	TBD	$4.00
Salary vs. Budget	74%	TBD	41%
Starting Rate (Hr)	$11.00	TBD	$10.00 - $15.00
Repeat Call Tracking	No	Yes	Yes
IVR Usage	17%	30%	0%

Differentiation

Metric	Current	Competitor	Best Practice
Manager to Agent Ratio	1:18	1:16	1:15
Agent Certification	No	Yes	NA
Turnover	7.5%	2-4 Agents/month	8%
Part Time agents	0%	40%	35%

Table 8 - Comparative Matrix Example - Best Practice

Assessment Outputs

Having assessed each relevant area of focus and its respective properties during the discovery process, the next step is to analyze the findings and to define the perceived opportunities for improvement The following pages are intended to demonstrate some potential outputs from a full scale contact center assessment.

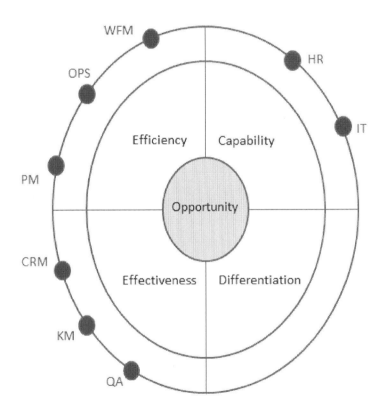

Considerations

There are several reasons why management may fund a contact center assessment, and clearly the outputs of the assessment must be tailored to fulfill those needs. If project sponsorship is undertaken by senior company management, most often the underlying goal is to understand how the center can play a more strategic role in the success of the business and/or how costs can be cut without adversely affecting customer acquisition and retention. If on the other hand, the sponsor is the individual responsible for contact center operations, the goal is often more tactical.

At that tactical level, the assessment outputs should focus on findings regarding efficiency (operations, process management, and workforce management), effectiveness (customer relationship management, knowledge management and quality assurance), capability (human resources and information technology) and competitive differentiation.

The results of interviews, observations, focus group sessions, data collection, and documentation evaluation can all be compiled and summarized together with any perceived opportunities for improvement in these specific areas. These outputs will give contact center management the necessary 'ammunition' to rectify functional issues. This in itself may satisfy the business case for the assessment, particularly when management were simply seeking verification of a particular issue and vindication for the course of action necessary to rectify that situation.

For strategic evaluation purposes, however, a summary of overall findings from a full scale contact center assessment could be demonstrated as follows:

- Competitive position and contact center role
- Operational analysis
- People Issues
- Technology Issues
- Process Issues
- Future Vision
- Integration
- Comparative Analysis

Outputs

The following pages describe how a contact center assessment might be presented at the highest level.

Competitive Position & Center Role	Issue/Finding	Implications/ Recommendations	Priority/ Time
Current Positioning	Competitive perception Quality v Price Key attributes	List changes required to current positioning based on issues and findings	
Current role of the Center	Customer perception Contribution to customer retention Strategic differentiation	List ways to support value added activities Quantitative ways to define value proposition	
Strategic Growth Plans	List value-added services 'as is' v. 'should be' Technology changes needed Customer segmentation Sales/service cohesion	Business planning	
Future Role of the Center	Customer data collection and warehousing Sales potential New technology testing	Potential to play strategic organizational role	
Summary & Action Plan	Senior management awareness of role Quantitative value definition Credibility issues	Develop strategic contact center plan with management Develop credible process management system	

Analyzing Operations	Issue/Finding	Implications/ Recommendations	Priority/ Time
Benchmark Comparison	Benchmarks surpassed/failed	Specific opportunities for improvement	
Workforce Management	Areas where agent utilization is subordinate	Alignment of breaks and schedules with historical peaks and valleys	
Other metrics	Focus on simple operational metrics	Complex metrics such as ROFC, Occupancy, and cost per contact	
Effectiveness	Focus on service rather than problem-solving	Customer satisfaction survey	

People Issues	Issue/Finding	Implications/ Recommendations	Priority/ Time
Performance	Quality Assurance one-dimensional	More diverse QA to include CRM, problem-solving and productivity	
Incentives	Impact of financial incentives	Clearer criteria for rewards and recognition Creation of new positions	
Employee Satisfaction	Changes to incentive and performance schemes	Common employee satisfaction surveys Focus groups Action plans	
Supervisor Analysis	Reduce fragmentation Provide better coaching	Minimize interruptions for routine contacts Reduce reporting Provide updated training	

Outputs

Technology Issues	Issue/Finding	Implications/ Recommendations	Priority/ Time
Automation	IVR not user friendly/ limited functionality	Increase IVR functionality and ease-of-use	
Contact Tracking	Absence of contact tracking is causing redundancy and customer irritation	Implement improved contact tracking capabilities.	
Knowledge Management	Agent inability to access relevant information in real time	Implement web-based knowledge management system Link KM with CRM	
Web & Social Media	Disparate customer sources and media capabilities	Unified communications and information oversight	

Process Issues	Issue/Finding	Implications/ Recommendations	Priority/ Time
Approach	Absence of process management team is counter-productive	Form team Conduct survey Identify key issues (customer perspective)	
Process Management Team	Balanced scorecard needed to track center performance	Team should represent center, have a champion, act autonomously	

Future Vision	Issue/Finding	Implications/ Recommendations	Priority/ Time
Evolve the center	Absence of process management team is counter-productive	Form team Conduct survey Identify key issues (customer perspective)	
Segment customers	Balanced scorecard needed to track center performance	Team should represent center, have a champion, and act autonomously	
Provide premium service	True value-added service for most profitable customers	Identify strategic candidates Conduct studies to identify customer needs Offload routine tasks	
Integrating sales & service	Need to improve hand-offs from customer service	Either train agents to handle new clients or hand-off to inside sales	
World Class Service	Center has the opportunity to meet several benchmarks	Use process management techniques New multi-media technology integration Premium services Value-added services included More defined career paths for agents Service and sales closely integrated Center provides strategic information Center uses a recognized balanced scorecard approach.	

Output Example

The following is an example of a detailed output using one of the high-level opportunities for improvement identified previously, as follows:

Technology Issues	Issue/Finding	Implications/ Recommendations	Priority/ Time
Contact Tracking	Absence of contact tracking is causing redundancy and customer irritation	Implement improved contact tracking capabilities.	

Detail:

Enhancement	Scenarios
Retrieval of multi-channel customer transaction history	▪ Customer refers specifically to previous call, e-mail, fax or postal mail contact ▪ Customer calls back several times regarding time of pick-up or delivery ▪ Customer has spoken to company previously and agent needs to refresh his/her memory or acknowledge previous contact ▪ Customer is using the company web site and has an inquiry or problem ▪ Customer has spent several minutes attempting unsuccessfully to use the IVR
Contact categorizations	▪ Contact categorizations are derived from existing knowledge of why customers contact the company ▪ Agent has the ability to rapidly select the contact type and (sub) detail from a list ▪ Agent can optionally use the selected contact type and detail to trigger an automatic search of existing SOPs, thus ensuring consistent customer interaction ▪ Agent can prioritize the contact and assign a status based on the need (if any) for follow-up work ▪ Agent can dispatch or escalate a contact from the desktop to individuals or groups with a need to know (e.g., sales lead) ▪ Users can manually define and create records for multi-channel customer contacts, thus

Enhancement	Scenarios
	creating an "end-to-end" customer interaction history • System can link to multi-channel contacts such as e-mail, stored faxes, imaged mail, IVR records, or web site interactions
Integration with enterprise systems	• Contact tracking system can be rapidly integrated with planned enterprise systems. This is critical for database interactions via the customer master file, sales force automation tools and other key functions, in order to eliminate redundant data entry, reduce average handling time, and enhance customer relationship and management reporting capabilities
Integration with knowledge management systems	• Contact tracking system can initiate interaction with online documentation or knowledge-based system based on previous contact history or automatic/manual keyword search.
Advanced CTI integration	• Contact tracking system automatically logs user interaction and time spent using any IVR functions. This provides agents with immediate insights as to customer need as well as creating records for management reporting purposes • Based on web – call center integration (currently unavailable), contact tracking system captures customer Internet access at the time of contacting the customer service center • Unified messaging capabilities enable agents to handle inbound e-mails, faxes, imaged mail, etc., as separate contacts
Creation of user privilege classes	• Based on privilege class, user may access differing levels of information pertinent to contact tracking system needs. For example, certain individuals view certain contact types and details, and may access privileged commercial and off-label account management data. • Privilege classes are used to dictate system administration, service, sales, marketing, and

Enhancement	Scenarios
	other access criteria.
Business rules for escalations & complaints	▪ The contact tracking system should enable the creation of "cases" that can be used to track an open customer issue throughout its life cycle ▪ Case handling should be controlled via business rules that "fire" based on pre-defined time frames. For example, a commitment that has not been met, an escalated complaint from a key customer that has not been closed, etc.
Proactive callback commitment tracking	▪ Any callback commitment to a customer should result in a timely on-screen, e-mail, cellular or pager notification to the responsible party
Customer key indicators	▪ Contact tracking system could, at a glance, indicate to the user: - Customer lifetime value (revenue stream / discount schedule) - Customer longevity - Customer sensitivity (complaint history / special handling)
Online scripting	▪ Contact tracking system should enable agents to optionally invoke an online scripting module which can be used to facilitate interaction on certain call types, such as emergencies, prospective orders, irate customer feedback, etc.
Online 'voice of the customer' surveys	▪ The system should include a brief customer survey module that will enable client-facing individuals to rapidly capture customer comments related to price, service level, billing, and so on.
Management reporting facilities	▪ The contact tracking system should immediately enable management to produce ad hoc and formal reports. As one example, at the contact center level, these could include the following: - Volume and percentage by contact type and detail - Billing disputes and adjustment amounts - Duration by call type and detail - Customer contact volume by channel

Enhancement	Scenarios
	- Time of day frequency by contact types
	- Repeat contacts by customer
	- Resolution on first contact rate
	- Average contact value
	- Sales leads generated
	- Agent durations by call type and detail
	- Escalations by agent
	- Missed commitments by agent
	- Outbound call frequencies to field
	- Unsolicited customer comments.

The following page shows a graphical representation of an assessment output relevant to customer relationship management.

CRM Strategy (High-level Design)

Input

Mngt | Mktg. | Regulator | Operations | Sales | Marketing

e.g. Focus Groups

Customer-Impacting Internal Processes
- Knowledge Management
- SOPs

Contact DB
- Special Handling
- Chronological Contacts
- Case Management
- Exception Reports
- Business Rules

Master DB

Individual Customer DB

Firewall

Operational Layer (Section

Education and Retraining

Client Data Repository
(Sample Business Drivers)
- Compliance
- Equipment
- Personnel
- Policy Issues
- Price
- Requests
- Suggestions
- Competition
- Trends

Analysis
- Root Cause Analysis
- Trending
- Business Impact
- Financial Analysis

Management Reports

Enterprise System

135

ROI Analysis - Example

Risk Adjusted ROI = (Benefits/Cost) X Probability of Success.

This equation allows differentiation between solutions not only on the basis of cost, but also based on the likelihood of achieving the benefits associated with those costs.

Benefits

In general, the benefits a CRM system can deliver contribute to the bottom line in a few different ways:

- Increased revenues
- Decreased costs
- Deferred costs.

Here are a few focal points:

Sales/Marketing:

- Increased average value of transactions
- Reduced length of sales cycles (increased number of transactions)
- Improved close rates
- Increased percentage of time involved in sales activities
- Reduced costs for generating contacts (and handing them off to sales).

Customer Service:

- Reduced average number of calls to resolve a situation
- Reduce average time per call
- Increased customer satisfaction (increased customer loyalty).

Additional Benefits:

- Improved utilization of resources (load balancing)
- More precise product pricing
- Reduced printed literature costs
- Improved ability to grow revenue through strategic channels
- Improved communication between account team members
- Improved ability to develop products addressing customer/prospect needs.

Outputs

- Cost savings associated with Web service technologies.

The following information could also be used to develop a high level ROI analysis.

Sales:

- Annual company revenues
- Average transaction value
- Average revenue per inside sales representative
- Average length of sales cycle
- Average close rate on opportunities
- Number of inside sales reps using the system
- Average number of calls/month per inside sales rep
- Hours/month spent by inside sales on developing forecasts
- Hours/month spent by sales manager on rolling up forecasts
- Hours/month spent by inside sales on call reports
- Hours/month spent by inside sales on reviewing call reports
- Hours/month spent by inside sales reviewing accounts
- Hours/month spent by sales management reviewing accounts.

Marketing

- Number of marketing projects per year, categorized by type (print ad, broadcast ad, mailing lists, trade shows, seminars)
- Average cost for each of these types of campaigns.

Customer Service

- Average burdened cost per agent
- Number of agents using the system
- Average number of contacts required to resolve a service incident (can break these down by type of contact if necessary)
- Average time per contact (on-phone, prep, follow-up, etc.)
- Average number of contact/month handled by each agent
- Number of existing customers
- Average yearly revenue per customer
- Average number of customers discontinuing service per month
- Number of sales referrals being generated per agent per month

Costs

The following should be considered in determining the Total Cost of Ownership for a CRM system:

- Initial purchase price of software
- Cost of adding modules (if applicable) at a later date
- Annual fees for maintenance, updates and technical support
- Implementation cost (both initially and incrementally as the business evolves)
- Administration costs.

Probability of Success

Factors influencing the probability of success are product architecture, implementation approach, and the partnership that a solution vendor offers. Key considerations might include:

- Vendor references
- Vendor investment in understanding customer business needs
- Executive management participation
- Proper expectation setting and planning
- Implementation by vendor or 3rd party
- Match with vendor culture
- Customer service.

Comparative Analysis

The contact center assessment comparative analysis is geared towards numeric outputs from the assessment findings. The goal here is to succinctly define the 'as is' and 'should be' states, as well as any definable ROI and/or benchmark data that may have been derived during the assessment.

Human Performance:

#	Function	Current	OPI	ROI	Benchmark
1	**Operating Environment**				
	Real Time Statistics				
	Turnover				
	Part Time Agents				
	Supervisor to Agent Ratio				
	Senior Agent to Agent Ratio				
	Closed Key Time				
	Gender Ratio				
	Skills-based Routing				
	Ergonomics				
2	**Metrics**				
	ASA				
	Abandonment				
	Occupancy				
	ATT				
	ACW				
	Availability				
	AHT Exceptions				
	Service Level (Av.)				
	Hold Tracking				
	Transfer Tracking				
	In/Out Call Ratio				
	ROFC				
	% of Customer Base				
	Customer Satisfaction				

#	Function	Current	OPI	ROI	Benchmark
	Customer Loyalty				
	Cost Per Call				
	Cost Per Agent				
	Salary vs. Budget				
	Average Starting Rate				
3	**Training**				
	CSR Certification				
	System Design				
	On-the-job Training				
4	**Supervisory**				
	Performance (CMS) Training				
	Escalations				
	Field Coordination				
	Career Path				
5	**Quality Assurance**				
	Average CSR Score				

Process

#	Function	Current	OPI	ROI	Benchmark
6	**Sales**				
	Special Handling				
	Special Customers				
	Perceived Contact Center Accountability				
	Report of Calls Handled vs. Transferred				
7	**Inside Sales**				
	Relationship to Contact Center				
	Contact center Sales Lead Generation				
8	**Outsourcing**				
	Operational efficiency				
	Customer sat.				

Outputs

Information Technology

#	Function	Current	OPI	ROI	Benchmark
9	**IT**				
	CTI				
	Escalation Tracking				
	Call Tracking				
10	**IVR/Telephony**				
	IVR Usage				
	Caller Menu				
	Key Response				
	Script Interpretation				
	Queue Time				
	Repeat IVR Option				
	Voice Recognition				
	Advance Keying				
	800 Number				
	CSR Announcement				
11	**Knowledge Management (KM)**				
	Online Documentation				
	Troubleshooting				
	Service Intranet				
12	**Internet**				
	Call Offload				
	Internet Chat				
	Internet Callback				

CRM

#	Function	Current	OPI	ROI	Benchmark
13	**CVA**				
	Customer Satisfaction Surveys				
	Customer Profiling				
	Service Culture				
14	**Employee Satisfaction**				
	Compensation				
	Employee Sat Surveys				
	Career Path				
	Employee v. Customer Satisfaction Measure				
	Incentives				
15	**Social Media**				
	Frequency of Interaction				
	Number of Contacts to Resolution				
	Quality of Issue Resolution				
	Cost per SM customer				
16	**Customer Segmentation**				
	Personalized Service				
	Segmentation Strategy				

Other Output Examples

Customer Satisfaction Survey

S1. May I please speak with…

[CONTACT NAME ON SAMPLE]? **[SKIP TO S2]**

> 1   Available **[CONTINUE]**
> 2   Not available **[ENTER NAME, CALLBACK TIME]**
> 3   Yes, gave name -- another location **[ENTER NAME &**
> **PHONE]**
> 4   Yes, no name given -- another location ....**[ENTER**
> **PHONE]**
> 5   No, refused
> **[TERMINATE]**

[ONCE CONNECTED]   Hello, my name is _____ with (Company Name).

S2. I understand that you called the (Company Name) Customer Service Center in the recent past. Is that correct?

> 1   Yes .... **[CONTINUE]**
> 2   No........................ **[TERMINATE]**
> 3   Don't Know.......... **[TERMINATE]**

We are currently conducting a survey with customers who use the (Company Name) Customer Service Center. Your honest opinions about your recent experiences with (Company Name) Customer Service Center will assist them in providing you with the highest quality service possible. Please know your responses will be kept strictly confidential.

Do you have a few minutes now or is there a more convenient time to call you back?

1	Yes, Continue	............[CONTINUE]
2	No, Callback	...............[ENTER NAME, CALLBACK TIME]
3	Refused	.....................[PRINT: *"Your input is very valuable to (Company Name) and would be greatly appreciated."*

IF RESPONDENT STILL REFUSES, TERMINATE]

Please note that this call could be monitored or taped for quality assurance purposes.

1. What was your reason for calling the (Company Name) Customer Service Center?

   [READ RESPONSES]

2. Now, considering your recent experience with the (Company Name) Customer Service Center, including the people that you dealt with and the service you received, how would you rate your **Overall Satisfaction** with your experience?

   Please use a 7-point scale where a "1" means you are **Extremely Dissatisfied** and a "7" means you are **Completely Satisfied**, and you may use any number in between.

Extremely Dissatisfied					Completely Satisfied		DK
1	2	3	4	5	6	7	8

[IF Q1 = 1, 2, OR 3, ASK Q1A.   IF Q1 > 3, SKIP TO Q2]

3. Why do you feel this way?   **[PROBE: *"Anything else?"*]**

144

4.　Please continue to use the same rating scale where a "1" means **extremely dissatisfied** and a "6" means **completely satisfied**, to rate your level of satisfaction with your experience with the customer service center on each of the following service attributes.　How satisfied are you that (Company Name) customer service center agent... **[RANDOM START AND ROTATE A-J]**

	Dissatisfied				Satisfied
a. Answered your call promptly	1	2	3	4	5
b. Correctly recognized your company's name and address	1	2	3	4	5
c. Recognized and understood your inquiry or problem	1	2	3	4	5
d. Cared about resolving your inquiry or problem	1	2	3	4	5
e. Answered your questions clearly	1	2	3	4	5
f. Answered your questions accurately	1	2	3	4	5
g. Transferred you only when needed	1	2	3	4	5
h. Transferred you to the right person	1	2	3	4	5
i. Was friendly and courteous	1	2	3	4	5
j. Completely resolved your inquiry or problem	1	2	3	4	5

Approximately how often do you call (Company Name) Customer Service Center? **[READ LIST]**

       1   Less than once a month
       2   Once a month
       3   Once a week
       4   More than once a week

May I please verify your name?   **[ENTER NAME:**

     _____**]**

May I please verify your phone number -- **[PRINT PHONE NUMBER HERE]**. Is this correct?

       1   Yes .... **[SKIP TO CLOSE]**
       2   No .... **[PRINT: *"What is your phone number?"* ENTER PHONE NUMBER]**
       3   Refused .... **[SKIP TO CLOSE]**

[CLOSE]

That's all the questions I have for you today. I really appreciate your time and valuable input. Have a great day!

[RECORD GENDER -- DO NOT ASK]:
- Male
- Female
- Can't tell from voice

Employee Satisfaction Survey - Example

The effectiveness of a contact center is obviously affected by the attitude of the employees who staff it. Conducting an employee satisfaction survey is one way of determining opportunities for improvement in this regard.

Employee satisfaction surveys could be broken down into the following categories:

- Immediate management team (i.e., favoritism, treats with respect, keeps one informed, resources, etc.)
- Manager's boss (i.e., how does he/she communicate with me, do I have confidence in them, etc.)
- Company as a whole (i.e., pay, benefits, safe environment, do rules interfere with the job, customer satisfaction and company improvements).

The following are some examples of questions that could be included in such a survey:

- I feel the company values employee satisfaction
- I have seen or been affected by favoritism
- Employees work well together at the contact center regardless of human differences
- I find it difficult to balance my work and social life
- I am bothered by too much pressure in my job
- Fear of reprisal inhibits me from taking independent action
- My performance on the job is evaluated fairly
- There is good teamwork at this company
- I have a voice in the decision-making process when changes are planned that will affect me
- People are treated with respect by this company, regardless of level
- I am doing something I consider worthwhile in my job
- I have the opportunity to assume increased responsibility
- I have sufficient opportunities to use or improve my skill level
- Management does a good job of communicating with people
- Management is interested in the well-being of those who work here
- Management will act on the problems identified by this survey

- Management generally understands the problems we face on our jobs
- Management provides a clear sense of direction
- My supervisor does a good job of building teamwork
- My supervisor is receptive to suggestions for change
- My supervisor manages people well
- My supervisor helps me improve the way I solve customer problems.

Team Support

- My group gets together to solve our problems
- We work towards clear and common goals
- The way we are organized helps us to perform effectively
- The atmosphere in my group helps me to be productive
- When necessary, the entire team gets together to resolve their problems.

Customer Service Provisioning

- Customers appreciate it when I offer them services that they may not actually request
- After dealing with a difficult customer or an emergency situation, I have enough time to compose myself
- Agents pride themselves in giving customers the attention and courtesy they deserve
- I always have enough time to listen to what customers have to say
- In most cases, I am empowered to resolve the customer's request
- I am often forced to put a customer on hold while I access information for them?
- I often have to seek supervisory authority to resolve issues
- I have the tools necessary to get the job done right.

Information Technology Support

- I have confidence in the information I get from our systems
- Our systems allow me to access information quickly
- Our systems allow me to process orders quickly
- Our systems are easy to learn
- The IVR system is helpful to customers

My Job

- I enjoy dealing with customers
- I feel rewarded when I make customers happy
- My initial training effectively prepared me to deal with customer problems
- The performance goals set for me help me to satisfy my customers
- I am fairly paid for the work I do
- Developing my skills is a high priority at this company
- I am ultimately responsible for my own career development.

Additional Outputs

Some contact center assessments involve not only mainstream operational concerns, but also considerations of elements such as ergonomic design. Sometimes, the assessment may actually involve recommendations pertaining to the physical construction of the contact center.

Consider the following examples of findings from these types of assessment:

1. Multi-media and peripherals contribute to high noise levels at the customer service center. It is recommended that, where feasible, noise inhibiting features in service center design (white noise machines, sound absorbent tiling, carpeting, wallpaper, acoustic paneling, etc.) should be included at the new service center.

2. High-walled cubicles inhibit agents' ability to communicate easily. By adopting a center core agent pod design (3-6 workstations per pod), Agents will be able to exchange information using a conversational voice pitch, while still maintaining a degree of privacy.

3. It is recommended that the contact center environment should utilize both task and ambient lighting to create a comfortable working atmosphere. Use neutral tone carpeting and light wall coloring. Move agents as close as possible to natural lighting in order to conform to what are considered call center best practices in terms of design.

4. Enable agents to view customer service metrics, news releases, etc., from their workstations. This can be achieved by strategically placing metric wallboards and text reader boards around the customer service center.

5. Migrate hard copy work aids (cheat sheets, schedules, directories, etc.) to an online knowledge management system. This will alleviate wall space constraints that may occur as a result of center core design, as well as creating an aura of consistency from one

workstation to another.

6. Design the new customer service environment to allow for ergonomic peripheral placement and adequate storage areas. Again, this will highlight the design strengths of the center, rather than illuminate any potential for unsightly storage and inventory.

Contact Center Design Guidelines

Site

Answer the four major questions regarding site design:

1 – How long before the contact center must be operational?
2 – How large will it ultimately be?
3 – What must the look of the center be?
4 – What functionality must it have?

Considerations:

- What is the intended look of the building/contact center?
- How big will the center be? – know the targeted ultimate size of the center and who will occupy it.
- Lease and remodel, buy and remodel, or build to suit
- Know the local building codes regardless of choice – variance may be required for certain changes
- Consider emergency generators, external storage areas, waste containers, etc. Many of these issues can take extended time and effort to resolve
- Lease - calculate real square footage charges
- Understand occupied space vs. common charges (hallways, cafeteria, security, atrium, etc.)
- Be clear about what construction is allowed and can be accomplished reasonably
- Negotiate for landlord to perform code updates (ADA code, fire safety, hazmat removal, etc.)

- Have an independent, comprehensive inspection performed before signing a lease
- Sign as long a lease as possible – use as a bargaining point for lease terms
- Real Estate agency support - (do some legwork and ask questions)
- Evaluation matrix - the attribute point system
- Square footage
- Employee resource pool available – immediate & ongoing replenishment
- Utilities
- Current capacity
- Growth & upgrade potential – with current structure & expansion plans
- Reliability – Failure rates, average time to repair, customer service prioritization
- Diversity routing/multiple feeds available?
- Goods & services available - professional, police/fire/EMT, eating places, hotels,
- Snow removal, grounds maintenance, etc.)
- Transportation, (mass transit, taxi, highways, airports)
- Parking – employee, visitor, disability
- Quality of life – (setting, foliage, outdoor tables, noise levels, views, etc.)
- ADA code compliance & restrictions – (ramps, elevators, parking, etc.)

Infrastructure

- Sized for growth – what is the targeted ultimate population of the center?
- Contiguous/non-contiguous space, multiple floors, internal walls (permanent or temporary?)
- Effects management span of control, team continuity, workflow, etc.
- Safety considerations – sprinklers, fire escapes, outdoor lighting, hazmat, etc.
- Reflective coating on windows?
- Loading dock – available/secure?
- Freight elevator – available/shared? – prevents wear & tear on finished center

- HVAC capacities?
- Can the systems support the increased demand?
- Modification may be required as a result of planned new walls, cubicles
- Cable routing
- Spare capacity – How much abandoned cabling?
- Embedded ducts
- Raised floor
- Plenum routing, walls
- Emergency power – utility provided alternate feeds, generators, battery backup.
- Natural & artificial lighting – window, anti-glare baffles, incandescent desk light)
- Noise levels and abatement – (carpeting, glass walls, doors, offices, etc.)
- Facilities – (restrooms, cafeteria, vending, break rooms w/ electric & water service)
- ADA code compliance – aisle width, restroom layout, door handles, etc.
- Signage – Illuminated EXIT signs, room, office, cubicle numeric addresses, nameplates.

Workspace

- Functional layout (general groupings – agents, administration, etc.)
- Determine individual space allocation according to work
- Open plan/cubicles/offices? – for managers/agents – (pros/cons)
- Cubicles vs. center core design
- Individual/paired/quads? – wall height – seated privacy, full-height-(pros/cons)
- Heavy print requirements – printer per individual or shared?
- Shelf space/file cabinets for reference material, software, work folders, etc.
- Ergonomics – (Maximize desktop area, equip. positioning, monitor size, anti-glare/radiation screens, keyboard types & rests, chairs, headsets, telephone handsets, etc.)
- Individual workspace design and layout – maximizing space and utility

- Locating shared resources – printers, fax, copiers, etc.
- Color coordination – living with the choices.
- Team involvement in design – (pros/cons)
- Rules of the Road - Policy Statements and Guidelines re: living conditions
- What's allowed in the workplace - posters, music, etc.?

Ergonomic Design Considerations

Studies have shown that agents consider the following to be of prime concern in terms of designing work areas:

- The need to interact and communicate effectively
- Air quality and temperature conditions
- A space that allows people to concentrate without excessive noise and other distractions
- Comfort
- Personal Safety.

Workstations

Many small contact centers employ a cluster principle. Desks are built around a center core to form a small circle of workstations. This enables several agents to use the same peripherals, such as a fax machine or printer, communicate more easily, and even share the same receiver for monitoring external operations. Sometimes small partitions are built between workstations to afford some agent privacy without eliminating the centralized core concept. Many contact centers purchase monitor/keyboard lift trolleys to allow agents to stand up and still perform system tasks. Adjustable keyboards, work surfaces, mouse pads and monitor heights are especially useful in a shift environment. Electronic and power cabling is typically built into the workstation design.

On the down side, the cluster principle decreases agent privacy and prevents agents from personalizing their workspace (thus contributing to employee dissatisfaction). One study even found that agent workspaces surrounded on three sides by higher than standing eye-height actually improved cross-center communications. The same study found that a reduction of the workspace area by more than 25% generally decreases job satisfaction.

Noise

Surveys of existing contact centers have determined that excessive noise can be correlated with decreased job satisfaction and increased on-the-job stress and error rates. The use of white noise machines, as well as acoustic paneling, and sound absorbent carpeting, wallpaper and ceiling tiles can assist.

Lighting

High volume contact center employees rarely enjoy a sense of comfort. However, studies have shown that a combination of indirect or ambient lighting (such as parabolic lights or fixtures whose lighting is directed towards the ceiling), and task lighting (such as desk lamps) for hard copy reading and keyboard entry.

Many contact centers use natural light for agents where possible, allowing representatives to sit near windows (this has no documented correlation with job satisfaction), while supervisors, who tend to spend far less time at their desks, occupy the central floor area. Also, the choice of color is considered important, with a preference for light colored walls and earthy toned carpeting.

Seating

OSHA (Occupational Health and Safety Association) recommends chairs that permit easy adjustments to height and backrest angle. Some chairs automatically adjust to the weight of the agents.

Ancillary Areas

Many contact centers ensure that a dedicated team meeting, training and/or 'nesting' room is located in close proximity to the actual operation. This enables the manager or supervisor to monitor, train and brief agents without disrupting workflows. Such areas are typically wired for overflow calls and systems interaction. Also, in cluster principle workstation environments, it is considered important to provide a private area for agents to make telephone calls. Some centers ensure that water coolers are located close to agent work areas.

Other Considerations

Ergonomic vendors provide state-of-the-art contact centers with add-ons such as workstation air filters that re-circulate and purify air, helping to control room temperature in an environment where many agents are working in close proximity. These vendors also produce workstations that allow the positioning of monitors at an eye-to-screen distance of more than 30 inches, and at a 30-45 degree angle beneath the work surface.

Conclusion

Regardless of whether or not this book is used as the basis for a full-scale assessment, it has served its purpose if it finds a place on a customer care manager's bookshelf and is utilized as a quick reference guide or refresher on best practice approaches to any contact center classification.

As mentioned from the outset, no one publication dealing with a subject matter so broad can possibly hope to cover all of the contingencies surrounding contact center operations. For example, the area of workforce management alone is worthy of volumes of explanation when it comes to best practices. By providing broad but relevant questions and outputs, the goal here is to identity 'pain points' and provoke ideas on how to solve problems or implement improvements.

What is very apparent from dealing with contemporary contact centers is that apart from fundamental operational metrics, no two environments are exactly the same, whether because of the product or service offered, front line agent job responsibilities, management expectations, customer nuances or field involvement. There is no 'one size fits all', unless of course a company decides – as is often the case - to force-fit the contact center into a sanitized model that is motivated on a day-to-day basis purely by average speed of answer, abandonment rate and average talk time.

There are so many aspects to consider when it comes to the contemporary center environment, from quality assurance to operational efficiency, that it is too easy to lose sight of the strategic vision that is supposed to drive everyday behavior at the center in the first place, whether that is motivated entirely by cost or a desire to meet the customer's needs. Hopefully, by pulling all of these disparate business motivators together in more detail than is normally available, this publication will provide something for every professional tasked with operating such a complex environment.

Glossary

Automatic Call Distributor (ACD)   An ACD not only analyzes
and distributes high volumes
of inbound customer calls to
agents, but also captures and
stores extensive information
relevant to those calls.

After Call Work (ACW)   ACW refers to that work
which the agent must
accomplish in order to
satisfactorily conclude the
previous customer contact,
such as a billing
reconciliation, complex
notation, correspondence,
etc.

Automatic Number Identification (ANI)   ANI is a telecommunications
feature which enables the
recipient to view the
originating telephone number
before accepting the call.

Applications Programming Interface (API)

An Applications
Programming Interface
enables disparate computer
applications to interact
seamlessly by initiating
functions and sending and
receiving data.

Glossary

Average Speed of Answer (ASA)

ASA usually refers to the time lapse between a call being received (or the caller selecting a prompt) and an agent accepting the call

Average Talk Time (ATT)

Average Talk Time refers to the average amount of time an agent or group of agents are taking between accepting and terminating a particular inbound call.

Automated Attendant

Automated Attendant delivers a pre-recorded message, but also asks the caller to select their agent preference from a pre-defined list of choices.

Automated Data Gathering

This term refers to the ability of a system to gather information relevant to a particular user transaction in a consistent and useful manner. For example, an integrated system might capture a billing transaction, while also gathering information regarding a product problem resolution without agent intervention.

Content Improvement Team (CIT)

The goal of any customer service Content Improvement Team is to ensure that relevant, accurate and complete online information is available to users (agents and customers) in a timely manner.

Glossary

Computer-Telephony Integration (CTI)   CTI refers to the marriage of computer functions with telecommunications in order to retrieve, process and store information relevant to an inbound telephone call (such as automatically matching a customer contact record to an inbound number before the agent accepts the call).

Dialed Number Identification Service (DNIS)

DNIS is a telephony function which enables inbound calls to be routed according to the number dialed. This is particularly useful for a contact center with discrete toll-free numbers for different functions.

Help Desk   The help desk is the correlate to the contact center in that its function is to resolve customer inquiries and problems. Unlike the contact center, however, the help desk handles *internal* customer contacts, which typically involve technological issues.

Interactive Voice Response (IVR)   Interactive Voice Response describes computer software that is designed to enable customers to access certain types of information, via the telephone, without having to reach an agent (e.g., checking account balance, etc.).

Glossary

Knowledge Engineering (KE)

Knowledge engineering originally referred to complex artificial intelligence programming. Today, it is often used to describe the task of construing solutions to user problems and inputting this information into an existing knowledge base "shell" for manipulation by an intelligent troubleshooting system.

Local Area Network (LAN)

A Local Area Network is usually comprised of a group of adjacent computers which share common resources, such as software applications.

Quality Improvement Team (QIT)

In the context of this book, the goal of a Quality Improvement Team is to identify any contingency which may inhibit the efficient resolution of a customer contact, such as a process, system or content deficiency.

Resolution On First Contact (ROFC)

The primary goal of any customer service environment is to provide mechanisms which enable any relevant inbound contact to be satisfactorily resolved without need for any further interaction with the customer on that matter.

Glossary

Service Level

A contact center service level refers to the average number of inbound calls which are being accepted by agents within a given time frame. A traditional industry standard, for example, is the goal of answering "80% of calls within 20 seconds".

Skills-based Routing

Skills-based routing is an ACD feature which enables inbound calls to be routed to the agent best qualified to deal with the type of inquiry the caller has indicated (via prompts) he or she would like to make.

Speech Recognition

Speech recognition enables an inbound caller to respond to prompts using verbal, rather than keypad responses.

Total Quality Management (TQM)

An approach to management which evolved from W. Edwards Deming "Plan, Do, Check, Act" principles and was first used by the United States Department of Defense.

Index

Accessibility, 74

Analysis of Variance, 36

Assessment Outputs, 125

Capability, 85

Clarity, 75

Classifications, 26

Comparative Analysis, 140

Comparative Performance, 122

Customer Relationship Management, 65

Customer Satisfaction Survey, 144

Differentiation, 117

Discovery, 25

Ease of use, 75

Effectiveness, 63

Efficiency, 29

Employee Satisfaction Survey, 148

Glossary, 161

Human Resources, 87

Information Technology, 103

Glossary

Integration, 75

Integrity, 76

IVR, 107

Knowledge Management, 71

Operations, 31

Process Management, 51

Quality Assurance, 79

Relevance, 75

ROI Analysis, 136

Strategic Alignment, 17

Workforce Management, 41

Index

27022721R00092

Made in the USA
Lexington, KY
24 October 2013